Key Stage 3
Science

Practice Papers

Key Stage 3
Science

SATS Practice Papers

Levels 5-7

Great Value Pack Contains:

<u>Three</u> full sets of SATS practice papers
plus detailed answer book
(112 pages in all)

Key Stage 3

Science Test

Practice Paper 1A

Read this page, but don't open the booklet until your teacher says you can start. Write your name and school in the spaces below.

First Name *anita*

Last Name *sharma*

School

Remember

- The test is one hour long.
- Make sure you have these things with you before you start: pen, pencil, rubber, ruler, angle measurer or protractor, calculator.
- The easier questions are at the start of the test.
- Try to answer all of the questions.
- Don't use any rough paper — write all your answers and working in this test paper.
- Check your work carefully before the end of the test.
- If you're not sure what to do, ask your teacher.

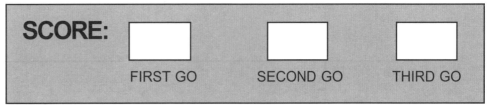

SCORE:			
	FIRST GO	SECOND GO	THIRD GO

1. (a) Investigations show that oak trees take water and oxygen from the soil.
Name **one** other **type** of substance a tree needs to take in from the soil.

..........*minerals*..........

1 mark

(b) The roots of an oak tree are long and split up into smaller roots.
Explain how this helps the tree take in water.

has larger surface area, to absorb
more water

1 mark

(c) Oak trees lose their leaves in winter.
How does this stop the tree growing?

leaves are needed to photosynthesis,
without leaves theres no food for tree

1 mark

(d) This picture shows a caterpillar
which feeds on oak leaves.
Describe how the caterpillar's
appearance helps it survive.

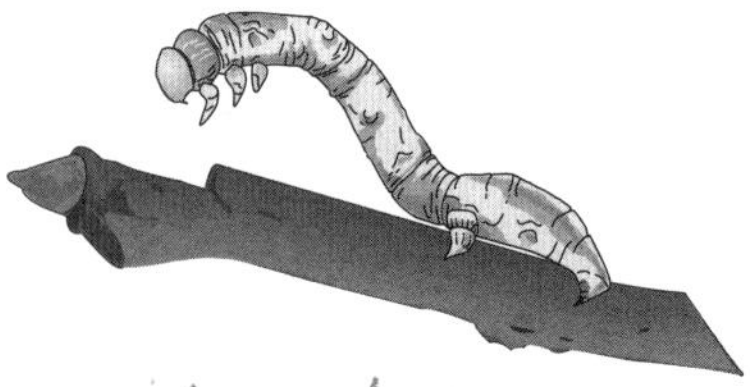

Its appearence can easily be
camoflaged to the tree which keeps
it unoticed from predators

2 marks

maximum 5 marks

2. (a) Mr Ferrari wanted to know how much air he breathed out in one breath. He put water into a bell-jar, and put the bell-jar upside down in a container of water. The bell-jar had a scale on the side marked in ml.

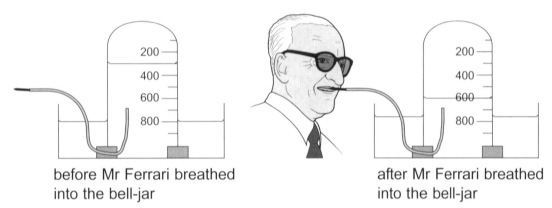

before Mr Ferrari breathed into the bell-jar

after Mr Ferrari breathed into the bell-jar

(i) What volume of air did Mr Ferrari breathe out? ....250...... ml

0

1 mark

(ii) Air is made up of nitrogen, oxygen, carbon dioxide, water vapour and noble gases.

The composition of the air that Mr Ferrari breathed in was different from the air he breathed out.
Write down **three differences**.

Compared to the air he breathed in, the air which he breathed out contained:

1. *more CO_2*   2. *more water vapour*

3. *little O_2*

3

3 marks

(b) In the picture below, tube X is labelled, which connects the lungs to the mouth.

tube X

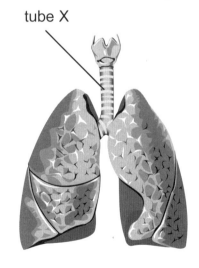

(i) Give the name of tube X.

....trachea...........

1

1 mark

(ii) The wall of tube X contains 'rings' of cartilage, a stiff material. Write down **one** function the 'rings' of cartilage might have.

To help support the cartilage

1

1 mark

maximum 6 marks

3. **Cirrhosis** is the name for a type of damage to the liver. It is caused by frequently drinking large amounts of alcohol and it can kill **quickly**. The graph shows the number of people in Germany who died from cirrhosis between 1970 and 2000.

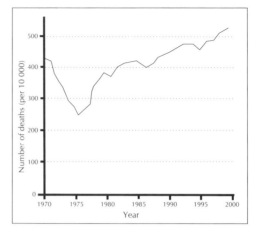

(a) Roughly in which year was alcohol in short supply?

1 mark

...19.7.5......

(b) Which one of these properties makes alcohol a **drug**? Circle the correct answer.

It's a chemical.

It's soluble in water.

It can provide energy.

It affects the nervous system. ✓

1 mark

(c) Look at this graph:

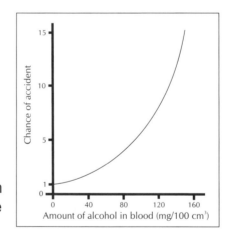

(i) Use the graph to describe how an increase in the amount of alcohol in the blood affects a person's chance of having an accident.

2 marks

...The more the amount of alcohol in blood the more chance of an accident...

....

(ii) Which of the following could explain why alcohol in the blood could cause accidents? Circle the correct answer.

Alcohol lowers body temperature.

Alcohol is a stimulant.

1 mark

Alcohol increases the time it takes for a person to react. ✓

Alcohol makes people happy.

maximum 5 marks

4. Suzanne is looking at a cup.
Light is shining onto the cup.

(a) Describe how light from the lamp lights up the cup so Suzanne can see it.

...light...from....the..lamp..light....shines...onto....

..cup..which....then...reflects..into...suzannes...

..eyes

2

2 marks

(b) Suzanne looks at different coloured cups in different colours of light.
Fill in the empty boxes in the table to show what colour the cups appear to her.

colour of cup	white	blue
colour of light	red	white
colour of cup to Suzanne	red	blue

2

2 marks

(c) Why does a black object look black in any light?

....Because...it...absorbs...all...colours

1

1 mark

(d)

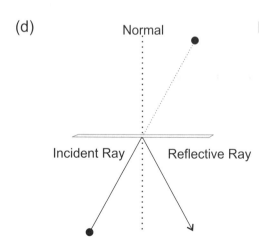

Normal

Incident Ray / Reflective Ray

In the diagram, measure the following:

(i) The angle of incidence

.........30°.........

(ii) The angle of reflection

.........30°.........

(iii) The distance from the object to the mirror

.........2.5cm.........

(iv) The distance from the image to the mirror

.........3cm.........

3

4 marks

maximum 9 marks

5. Four metals were added to cold water and to dilute hydrochloric acid. The results are shown in the table below.

metal	with dilute hydrochloric acid	with cold water
nickel	some bubbles of gas form if the acid is warm	no reaction
potassium	(cannot be done safely)	floats, then melts, a flame appears, and sometimes there's an explosion
platinum	no reaction	no reaction
zinc	bubbles of gas form and metal dissolves slowly	no reaction

(a) Write the names of the **four** metals in order of reactivity.

.....*Potassium*..... (most reactive)

.....*Zinc*.....

.....*nickel*.....

.....*platinum*..... (least reactive)

2

2 marks

(b) (i) Name another metal, that is **not** in the table, which reacts in a similar way to potassium. .....*Sodium*.....

1

1 mark

(ii) What is the gas which is formed when zinc reacts with dilute hydrochloric acid? .....*hydrogen*.....

Zn

1

1 mark

(c)   Two test tubes have been set up as shown in the diagram below.

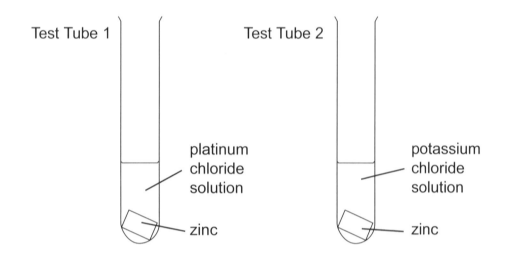

Test Tube 1   Test Tube 2

platinum
chloride
solution

potassium
chloride
solution

zinc   zinc

Nothing happened in Test Tube 2.
In Test Tube 1, the zinc was gradually covered with a grey deposit.

(i) **What** was the grey deposit that formed in Test Tube 1?

.....platinum.............................

(ii) Why did **no** reaction take place in Test Tube 2?

.....potassium...is...more...reactive...then...zinc

....

maximum 6 marks

6. This picture shows an archer.
He holds the arrow and pulls it back to fire it.

string bow

arrow

(a) At the moment shown in the picture, two **horizontal** forces act on the arrow:
the force exerted by the string and the force exerted by the archer's fingers.
The arrow **isn't** moving.

The archer pulls the arrow back and holds it with a force of 120 N.
Predict the force exerted by the string on the arrow.

.............60............. N

0

1 mark

(b) The archer releases the arrow and it moves forward. Explain why this happens.

...Because pressure of the arrow has...

...been released

0

1 mark

(c) While the arrow is flying across the field, **two** forces act on it. Gravity acts
downwards and air resistance acts in the opposite direction to the movement.
Explain why these forces **can't** balance each other, even if they are the same size.

...Because the arrow will land on the

...ground and gravity will be the only force

0

1 mark

(d) The arrow hits a target. The end of the arrow is pointed and sharp
so that it exerts a large pressure on the target.
Explain why a blunt end would exert a lower pressure on the target.

...Slightly more drag will act on it......

...has to be aerodynamic

0

1 mark

maximum 4 marks

7. This table shows information about the planets in the Solar System.
They are displayed in alphabetical order.

Planet	distance from the Sun (million km)	surface temperature (°C)	radius (km)	time for one rotation on axis (hours)	time for one orbit around Sun
Earth	150	+14	6378	24	365 days
Jupiter	778	-153	71 492	9.8	11.9 years
Mars	228	-55	3397	24.7	687 days
Mercury	58	+170	2440	1406	88 days
Neptune	4504	-225	24 766	16	165 years
Pluto	5914	-236	1137	153	249 years
Saturn	1429	-185	60 268	10.8	29.5 years
Uranus	2871	-214	25 559	17.3	84 years
Venus	108	+457	6052	5832	225 days

(a) Why is Pluto the coldest planet?

Because it is the furthest away
from the sun

1 mark

(b) There is no liquid water on the surface of Mercury or Mars.
Explain why.

Mercury closest to the sun, and is
to hot

1 mark

Mars is too cold to have a liquid.

1 mark

(c) Which planet has the shortest day? jupiter

1 mark

(d) What is the name of the force that keeps
the planets in orbit around the Sun? gravitational
pull

1 mark

(e) Explain why we can see the planets, even though they're not light sources.

The sun reflects light onto the planets
which then reflect light into our eyes

2 marks

maximum 7 marks

© CGP 2002

8. This diagram shows a woman's reproductive system before fertilisation.

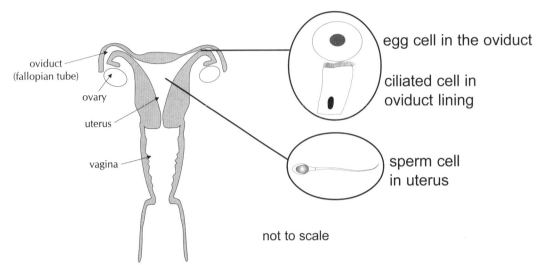

oviduct (fallopian tube)

ovary

uterus

vagina

egg cell in the oviduct

ciliated cell in oviduct lining

sperm cell in uterus

not to scale

(a) Cells from the oviduct were examined under a high powered microscope. They were found to contain ciliated cells. What is the function of ciliated cells?

Has hairs to filter out the egg cell from the oviduct

☐ 1
1 mark

(b) Video footage of fertilisation shows that the sperm cell fertilises the egg cell in the oviduct. Write down **one** way in which the sperm cell is adapted to its function.

Has a long tail to help swim to egg cell

☐ 1
1 mark

(c) Hens' eggs have a yolk. This yolk is a store of food for the developing chick. How does a human foetus get its food?

It gets its food from the parent by the umbilical cord and placenta.

☐ 2
2 marks

maximum 4 marks

9 (a) All of the following substances are included in a balanced diet:

fat   **starch**   **vitamins**
  minerals   **fibre**   **protein**

(i) Which two substances in the list are absorbed into the blood **without** being digested?

......*minerals* and ...*vitamins*.

2 marks

(ii) Which substance in the list passes through the body without being digested?

......*fibre*......

1
1 mark

(b) Rowan investigated the digestion of protein using **protease**, an enzyme. She kept the test tube containing the mixture of protein and protease in a water bath at 25 °C.

Why was the mixture kept in the water bath?

...To help the enzyme *protease* to work...

0
1 mark

This information describes how to perform a Biuret test:

> Add sodium hydroxide (NaOH) solution to the mixture.
> Then add drops of copper sulphate ($CuSO_4$).
> If protein is present, the solution turns from **pale blue** to **purple**.

Every **30 seconds** Rowan did a Biuret test on a drop of the protein and protease mixture.
Initially, the drops turned purple. After 180 seconds, they stayed pale blue.

(c) Why did the mixture stop turning purple after 180 s?

...Protien in the mixture was gone...

...after 180 s...

0
1 mark

(d) Rowan then did the experiment again with the water bath at 30 °C.
The drops stopped turning purple after 120 s.
How does increasing the temperature from 25 to 30 °C affect digestion of protein?

...The higher the temperature the less...

...protien there is to be digested...

0
1 mark

(e) Rowan wants to compare the results of the experiments at 25 °C with those from the experiment at 30 °C. What does she need to do to make it a fair test?

...Do the tests again...

0
1 mark

....

maximum 7 marks

10. Katie did an experiment with four liquids.
She secured cotton wool around the end of four thermometers.
A thermometer was then dipped into each liquid. When each
thermometer was removed, the temperature was recorded.
The temperature was then recorded every minute.

The table shows Katie's results:

Time (mins)	Thermometer reading (°C)			
	A	B	C	D
0	22	22	22	22
1	20	20	14	19
2	19	19	10	14
3	17	3	2	9
4	17	4	-3	4
5	16	5	-5	3
6	16	6	-8	2
7	15	7	-4	2
8	15	8	0	3
9	15	9	5	3
10	15	10	9	4
11	15	11	12	6
12	15	12	18	8

(a) Using the results, which liquid took
the shortest time to evaporate? ....D...........................

1 mark

(b) Using the results, which liquid took
the longest time to evaporate? ....A...........................

1 mark

(c) The reading on the thermometer dipped in liquid C went up after six minutes.
Explain why this happened.

.........It changed state at room temp...................

....

1 mark

(d) Write down the most likely temperature of the room Katie did the experiment in.

........20..... °C

1 mark

(e) Katie did the experiment again with liquid D. She dipped the thermometer
into the liquid **without** wrapping the bulb in cotton wool.
Write down two ways that her second set of results would be different.

.........She didn't wrap the bulb in cotton
wool and, she didn't repeat for other
liquids

2 marks

maximum 6 marks

11. Exploration by space probes on Mars shows that there are volcanoes, mountains and dry river channels on the planet.

(a) Mars has three types of rock: sedimentary, metamorphic and igneous. Explain how scientists used the information above as evidence for this.

> 2
> 3 marks

igneous rocks are found near volcanoes, metamorphic rocks are found near mountains, sedimentary rocks are found in dry rivers

(b) The space probes contain temperature sensors which suggest that the surface temperature on Mars ranges from -100 °C to 10 °C in the same day. Explain **how and why** this affects the rocks on the surface.

> 2
> 2 marks

It causes them to split into two, after it has frozen and warmed, expand and contracts, freeze thaw

12. The picture shows a heavy rotating wheel that can be used to store energy.

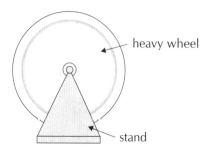

heavy wheel

stand

(a) Energy is transferred to the wheel to make it rotate.
What type of energy is the energy in the rotating wheel?
Circle the correct answer.

chemical energy   ~~kinetic energy~~   thermal energy

potential energy

1

1 mark

(b) The wheel is set rotating. When it reaches a high speed, no more energy is supplied to it. The wheel is connected to a dynamo. The dynamo turns, providing energy to light a bulb.

When the wheel stops rotating, the bulb goes out. Some of the energy stored in the wheel is **not** transferred to the bulb. List **two** places where energy is lost and explain how.

1. Sound energy, when it makes sound

2. thermal energy, heat is lost when its stopped ✓

1

2 marks

(c) A different light bulb is connected and the experiment is carried out again. The new light bulb gives out more energy per second. Describe how the new light bulb affects the motion of the wheel, compared to the one used in part (b). Explain your answer.

It gives out more energy causing the wheel to rotate more

1

2 marks

maximum 5 marks

13. Workers in a shoe factory use a tool to make holes in the leather.

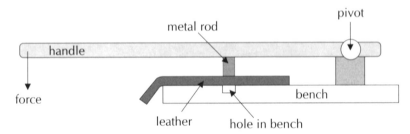

metal rod

pivot

handle

force

bench

leather   hole in bench

Not to scale

To punch a hole, a worker pushes the handle down. If the force is not large enough, the tool will not punch the leather.

A worker pushes on the handle with a force of 40 N.
The following diagram shows the force on the handle.

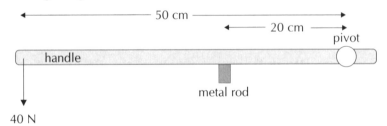

— 50 cm —

— 20 cm —

pivot

handle

metal rod

Not to scale

40 N

(a) Calculate the moment (turning effect) of the 40 N force applied to the end of the handle. Show your working and write down the units.

..............40 N ÷ 20 N = 20×100 = 200..............

.................= 200 N.IM²...............................

2 marks

(b) The moment pushes the metal rod onto the leather.
What force does the rod apply to the leather?

...gravity...

1 mark

(c) A different worker uses the punch.
The metal rod pushes on the leather with a force of 80 N.

(i) The end of the metal rod has an area of 0.5 cm². What pressure does the rod exert on the leather? Write down the units.

..........80 N ÷ 0.005 = 16000 N/M²..........

2 marks

(ii) This force is not great enough to punch through the leather.
How could the worker change the design of the tool so that it would punch with a force of 80 N on the handle?

....

....

1 mark

maximum 6 marks

Blank Page

Science

KEY STAGE
3

LEVELS
5-7

PRACTICE PAPER

1B

Key Stage 3

Science Test

46

Practice Paper 1B

Read this page, but don't open the booklet until your teacher says you can start. Write your name and school in the spaces below.

First Name _____

Last Name _____

School _____

Remember

- The test is one hour long.
- Make sure you have these things with you before you start: pen, pencil, rubber, ruler, angle measurer or protractor, calculator.
- The easier questions are at the start of the test.
- Try to answer all of the questions.
- Don't use any rough paper — write all your answers and working in this test paper.
- Check your work carefully before the end of the test.
- If you're not sure what to do, ask your teacher.

Exam Set SHP31

1. Wind power can be used to generate electricity using wind turbines like the one below.

Turbine turns

Wind

Sails turn

(a) As the wind spins the sails of the wind turbine, it turns a generator, which produces electricity.

Describe the useful energy changes which take place in this process.

The wind turns the turbine into kinetic energy, and the generator turns kinetic energy into electrical

2 marks

(b) Explain why wind is called a renewable energy source.

It never runs out, can be used again

1 mark

(c) Give two further examples of renewable energy sources that can be used to generate electricity.

1. Sun for solar power

2. Burning fossil fuels

1 mark

2 marks

(d) Greenpeace support the use of wind turbines rather than oil-fired power stations. Apart from cost, give **one** advantage and **one** disadvantage of an oil-fired power station over wind power.

advantage is renewable

disadvantage might not be as windy

2 marks

maximum 7 marks

2. On 9th Jan 2001 there was an eclipse of the Moon.

The diagram shows the positions of the Moon and the Earth.

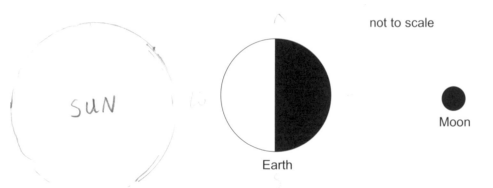

not to scale

SUN

Earth

Moon

(a) Draw in the position of the Sun in the diagram.

1 mark

(b) Complete the following description of the eclipse:

The Moon does not produce its own light, it reflects

the light of the ...Sun.......

The Moon orbits around the .earth.....

On the night of the eclipse, the Earth was between the Moon

and the ...Sun...... No light from the Sun could reach

the ..earth.. and it went dark.

2

3 marks

(c) The diagram shows half of the world in shadow. Explain why this half of the world does not stay dark all the time.

...Because the earth spins................................

....

1 mark

(d) The Sun rises in the East in the morning and sets in the West.
Looking down on the Earth from above the North Pole, which way does it spin?

......Clockwise...

0

1 mark

maximum 6 marks

3. Different metals expand at different rates when heated.

1 metre of metal heated by 10°C

Metal	aluminium	brass
Increase in length in mm	0.25	0.19

A bimetallic strip is two metal strips (one aluminium and one brass) fixed together. When heated it bends as shown below.

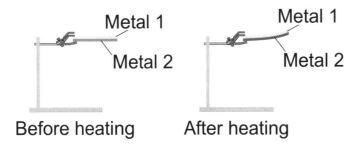

Before heating   After heating

(a) Identify which metal is the aluminium.

..metal 2...

1 mark

(b) In an experiment iron and steel are heated by 10°C.
1 metre of iron expands 0.12 mm and steel by 0.11 mm.

It is decided to replace the brass in the original strip to make it bend **more**. Suggest which metal should be used.

.............Steel...

1 mark

(c) A bimetallic strip is used in a thermostat for a fan.

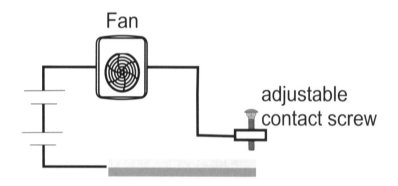

Fan

adjustable
contact screw

(i) When the temperature rises, the strip bends, the
circuit is connected and the fan turns on.
What happens as the temperature falls again?

...It becomes straught...

(ii) How is the screw used to control the temperature
when the fan turns on?

...Its stops the strip from bending...
...even more if its to hot...

maximum 4 marks

© CGP 2002

4. The diagram shows a crane lifting a block of concrete.
There are only two forces acting: the **tension** in the cable and the **weight** of the concrete.

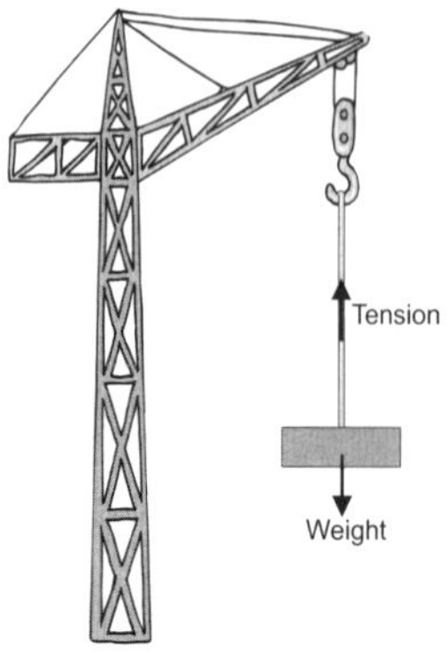

Look at these statements:

A: The tension is greater than the weight.
B: The tension is less than the weight.
C: The tension is equal to the weight.
D: There is not enough information to compare the forces.

Select the correct statement for each of the following situations:

(a) When the weight is being held without moving.

Statement ..D.. is true

0
1 mark

(b) When the weight is being lifted with increasing speed.

Statement ..A.. is true

1
1 mark

(c) The weight is still going up but is slowing down.

Statement ..B.. is true

1
1 mark

(d) The weight is travelling up with constant speed.

Statement ..C.. is true

1
1 mark

maximum 4 marks

5. Professor Cryer is investigating reactions of copper oxide.
Here is his description of what he did.

> I heated some dilute sulphuric acid in a beaker. Whilst stirring,
> I added copper oxide to it until no more would react. The mixture
> became a clear blue colour. I then filtered the mixture into a dish.
> A black solid was left on the filter paper. After a week, the liquid
> had gone and blue crystals were left.

Use this information to answer these questions:

(a) (i) What is the black solid left on the filter paper?

..............copper..........

1 mark

   (ii) What is the blue solution in the beaker?

..............Sulphur.........

1 mark

(b) Complete the word equation for the reaction which took place in the beaker

..Sulphuric.. + ..Copper........ → ...Sodeum.. + water
....acid......   oxide

1 mark

(c) Why did Professor Cryer need to filter the mixture?

.......To seperate the mixture..............................

....

1 mark

maximum 4 marks

© CGP 2002

6. Look at the following list of words:

carbon dioxide   sulphur dioxide

oxygen

copper oxide

carbon monoxide

nitrogen   carbon

(a) Name **three** elements from the words above:

1 _oxygen_

2 _nitrogen_

3 _carbon_

(b) Name **one** compound from the words above:

copper oxide

(c) Give the two compounds which are both formed from the same two elements.

1 _Carbon monoxide_

2 _carbon dioxide_

(d) Give the compound which traps heat to create the 'greenhouse effect'.

Carbon dioxide

(e) Give the gas which makes up most of the Earth's atmosphere.

nitrogen

(f) Give the gas responsible for acid rain.

sulphur dioxide

maximum 7 marks

7. Dieticians (diet experts) recommend that to get a balanced diet you must have all of these food types:

fats
proteins
vitamins
water
fibre

(a) (i) Give two food types that are provided well by eating fish.

1......*protien*......................

2.......*vitamins*...................

| 2 |
2 marks

(ii) Give two food types that are not provided well by eating fish.

1.......*fats*.........................

2.......*water*......................

| 1 |
2 marks

(b) Give two more food types not in the list needed for a balanced diet.

1......*carbohydrates*............

2............*minerals*.............

| 2 |
2 marks

(c) Food has to be chewed in order to obtain the nutrients.

Give two reasons why it is important to chew food.

1......*Easier to be digested, don't choke*......

2......*Can obtain all nutrients*......

....

| 1 |
2 marks

maximum 8 marks

8. Single celled organisms called dinoflagellates live in freshwater lakes.

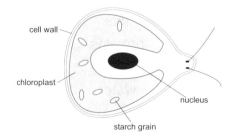

Use the cell diagram to answer these questions:

(a)   (i)   Is this organism more like a plant or animal cell?

...........*Plant cell*...........................

1 mark

(ii)   Explain your answer giving **two** examples.

1.........*Contains chloroplasts*...........................

2.........*has cell wall*...........................

2 marks

(b)   Another single celled organism called an amoeba traps and digests dinoflagellates.

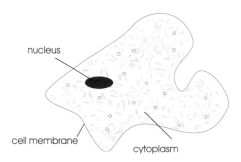

The amoeba's digestive enzymes break down the starch in the dinoflagellates.

Suggest what this process produces and what the product is used for.

....

....

....

2 marks

maximum 5 marks

9. The diagram shows a plank pivoted at one end.
A force of 100 N pushes up on the plank.

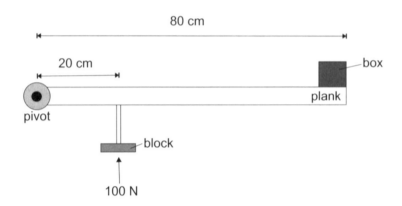

80 cm

20 cm ———— box

pivot

plank

block

100 N

(a) Calculate the moment (turning affect) of the 100 N force about the pivot.
Show your working.

100 N ÷ 20 cm = 500 N/M

| 0 |

3 marks

(b) The box is on the right hand end of the plank.
It is just heavy enough to keep the plank balanced.

| 0 |

1 mark

(i) What is the moment of the box about the pivot? Give the units.

100 ÷ 80 = 125 N/M

(ii) What is the weight of the box?

| 0 |

1 mark

125 N

(iii) The 100 N force acts on a block with area 5 cm². P. for
Calculate the pressure on the block. Give the units.

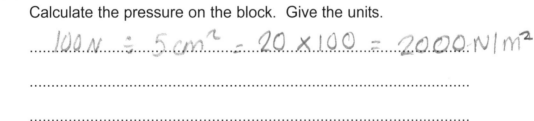

100 N ÷ 5 cm² = 20 × 100 = 2000 N/m²

| N |

2 marks

maximum 7 marks

10. Babs has two thermos flasks of water at 20°C. She heats two identical blocks of aluminium to 100°C and puts one into flask A and one into flask B.

The temperature of the water in each flask rises until it reaches a steady temperature. The table below shows Babs' results.

flask	temperature of water in °C at the start	temperature of block in °C at the start	volume of water in cm³	final temperature of water in °C
A	20	100	600	39
B	20	100	300	52

(a) Why is the final temperature of the water higher in flask B than in flask A?

It has a smaller volume of water

1 mark

(b) What is the final temperature of the two blocks of aluminium?

The block in flask A is at *39* °C.

The block in flask B is at *52* °C.

1 mark

(c) Which block of aluminium transferred more energy to the water? Explain your answer.

A, because has more water to transfer energy too

2 marks

maximum 4 marks

11. Michael has a toy submarine. It is hollow and water can flow in and out of it.
The submarine is in a sealed glass box, three quarters full of water.
Air can be pumped into or out of the box.
When air is pumped **in** the sub sinks. When air is pumped **out** it rises.

(a) When air is pumped **into** the tank what (if anything) happens to:

(i) the distance between the air molecules in the tank

...... are far apart ......

| 0 |
1 mark

(ii) the distance between the water molecules in the tank

...... are together ......

| 0 |
1 mark

(iii) the pressure of the air trapped inside the sub

...... it is high ......

| 1 |
1 mark

(iv) the volume of the air trapped inside the sub

...... is very little ......

| 1 |
1 mark

(b) Explain why the sub sinks down when air is pumped in.

...... The air molecules take the
...... room at the top, causing it
...... to sink ......

2 marks

maximum 6 marks

12. Banana plants grow in hot, dry countries. Because of the heat, soil can be hard and compact. Farmers spray water onto the soil around the trees.

(a) (i) Explain why only a small amount of water reaches the plant roots.

...Not...much...rain...fall...or...gets...

...evapourated...by...the...warmth...

1 mark

(ii) Give another reason why the hard, compacted soil makes it difficult for the banana plants to grow.

...Roots...will...find...it...hard...to...

...grow...

1 mark

(b) Plants need water. Give two reasons why this is true.

1....to...help...with...photosynthesis...

2....To...stay...alive...

2

2 marks

(c) A scientist suggests a new method for watering the plants.
The method involves digging a trench between the plants.
The trenches are filled with loosely packed rocks.
Water is piped into the trenches.

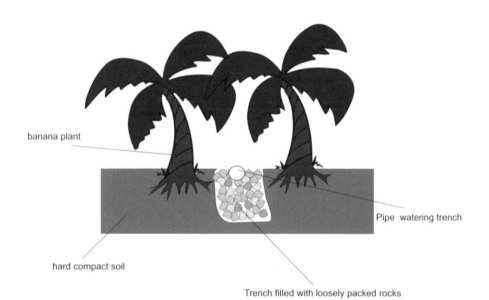

banana plant

Pipe watering trench

hard compact soil

Trench filled with loosely packed rocks

(i) Give **one** reason why the trenches are filled with rocks.

So that it won't get dried up when water falls into trenches

0

1 mark

(ii) The scientists also suggest adding nitrates to the water.
Give **one** reason why this will help the plants.

Gure nutrients to plant, to help grow

0

1 mark

maximum 6 marks

13. Complete the following table. The first one has been done for you.

Name	Formula or symbol	Compound / element	Structure diagram
Carbon dioxide	CO_2	compound	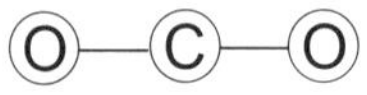 O—C—O
Oxygen	*O₂*	element	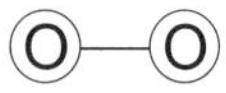 O—O
water *H₂O*		*compound*	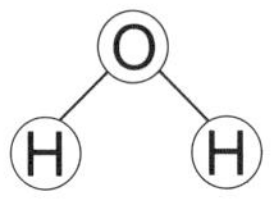 O H H
Sulphur	S	*element*	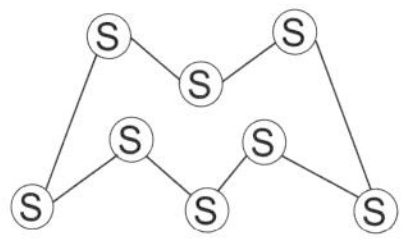 S S S S S S S S
Copper	Cu	element	 Cu
Sodium	Na	element	 Na
Carbon	C	element	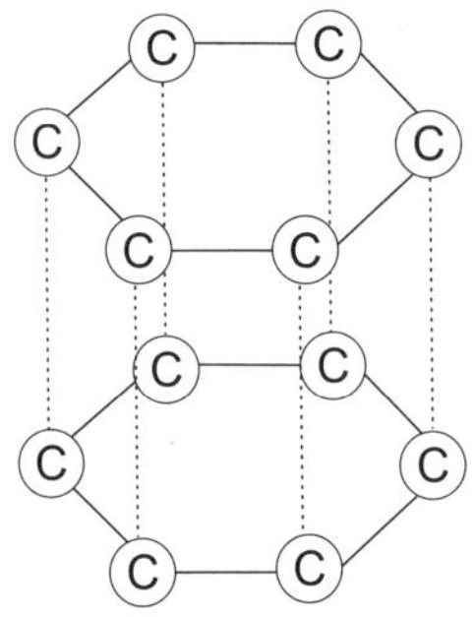 C C C C C C C C C C C C C C

1 mark

2 marks

1 mark

1 mark

1 mark

1 mark

maximum 7 marks

© CGP 2002

SHP3U

Key Stage 3

Science Test

Practice Paper 2A

Science

KEY STAGE 3

LEVELS 5-7

PRACTICE PAPER 2A

Read this page, but don't open the booklet until your teacher says you can start. Write your name and school in the spaces below.

First Name _Anitta_

Last Name _____

School _____

Remember

- The test is one hour long.

- Make sure you have these things with you before you start: pen, pencil, rubber, ruler, angle measurer or protractor, calculator.

- The easier questions are at the start of the test.

- Try to answer all of the questions.

- Don't use any rough paper — write all your answers and working in this test paper.

- Check your work carefully before the end of the test.

- If you're not sure what to do, ask your teacher.

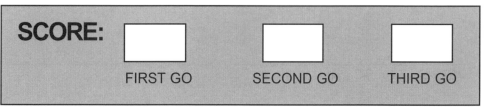

SCORE:		
FIRST GO	SECOND GO	THIRD GO

Exam Set SHP31

CGP

1. Plants need to take in water from the soil.
Dr Gabion decided to do an experiment to find out if there
is anything else in the soil which plants use for growth.

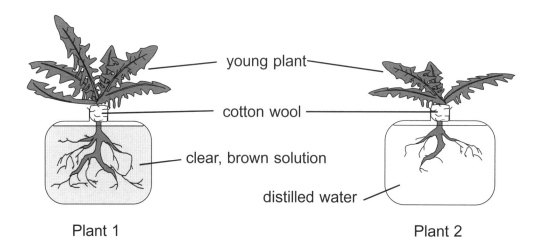

Plant 1   Plant 2

Dr Gabion made the clear, brown solution for Plant 1
by mixing up soil and water, and then separating the
soil particles out to leave the clear, brown solution.

(a) What method could Dr Gabion use to separate
the soil particles from the brown solution?

...... _Evapouration_ ....

∂

1 mark

(b) Why did Dr Gabion grow one plant in distilled water?

... _to see what will happen without_
..... _soil._ ....

0

1 mark

(c) (i) What type of substances are in the clear, brown
solution that the plant uses for growth?

... _minerals_ ...

l

1 mark

(ii) Explain how roots are adapted to take in water.

..... _they have a large surface area_ ....
..... _which helps with absorption_ ....

1

1 mark

(d)   Dr Gabion carried out another experiment with three similar plants.
The solutions in each container were the same. He put all the plants in
a sunny place. The pictures below show the result of the experiment.

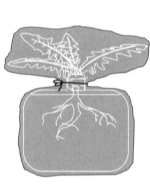

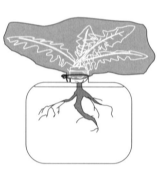

Plant 3

The container holds
the clear, brown
solution.
The container and
leaves are wrapped
in black plastic.

Plant 4

The container holds
the clear, brown
solution.
The leaves are
wrapped in black
plastic.

Plant 5

The container holds
the clear, brown
solution.
The container is
wrapped in black
plastic.

Of the three plants, Plant 5 was the only one which grew well.
Explain why.

It was able to absorb sun-light

for photosynthesis

1 mark

maximum 5 marks

2. Crushed ice at −30 °C was put in a dish. A thermometer was
placed in the ice, and the dish was heated gently for 15 minutes.

The graph below shows what the thermometer read during the 15 minutes.

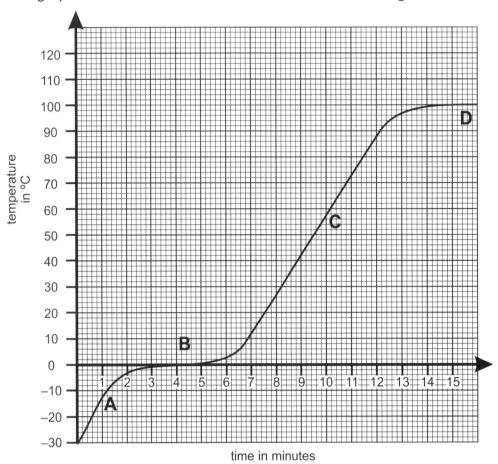

time in minutes

(a) How much did the temperature change in
the dish during the 15 minutes? ......130........ °C

☐ 1

1 mark

(b) Which letter on the graph shows:

(i) when the ice is melting? ...A.... (ii) when the water is boiling? ..C....

☐ 0

2 marks

(c) While the experiment was taking place, the dish and its contents were
removed from the heat quickly and weighed at the following times:

0 minutes   5 minutes   10 minutes   15 minutes

(i) At which **two** of the **times** would the weight measurements be the same?

......0......... minutes and ....5....... minutes

☐ 1

1 mark

(ii) Between which **two** of the times was the mass of
the contents of the dish changing most rapidly?

......5........ minutes and ......14........ minutes

☐ 0

1 mark

maximum 5 marks

3. Sahil did an experiment with the ink from blue, green and yellow felt-tip pens.
He coloured white paper strips with each pen and then dipped them into different
solutions. One solution was water, one solution had pH 1 and one had pH 10.

pH of solution	result with blue pen	result with green pen	result with yellow pen
1	turned purple	stayed green	stayed yellow
7	stayed blue	stayed green	turned orange
10	turned pink	turned yellow	turned red

(a) Which colour ink would make the most useful
indicator for acids **and** alkalis?
Explain your answer.

......Green pen.

> 0
> 1 mark

......Because green is neutral..

> 0
> 1 mark

Sahil coloured pieces of paper with each pen and then put them into some liquid.
He then put five drops of each coloured solution onto filter paper with a pipette.

The solutions spread out on the filter papers.
This diagram shows the papers after an hour.

(b) What is the name of this process of
investigating coloured substances?   ....Chromotography

> 1
> 1 mark

(c) Sahil made notes on the experiment.
Complete the paragraph by filling in the missing words.

> 1
> 3 marks

I made coloured solutions by putting coloured papers into the liquid. The solution

was coloured because a coloured substance had ....spread.... in the liquid.

This shows that the liquid is a ....solution.... for the coloured substances.

The filter paper experiment shows that only the ....green.... — coloured

pen probably contained two colours of ink.

maximum 6 marks

4. Five metals (1, 2, 3, 4 and 5) were investigated to see how they react in water. The tubes below show them reacting.

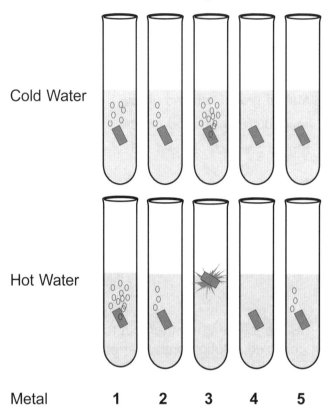

Cold Water

Hot Water

Metal   **1**   **2**   **3**   **4**   **5**

(a) Complete this prediction about the reactivity of the metals.

I predict that the most reactive metal *will be 3*

....

0

1 mark

(b) Using the pictures above, arrange the metals in order of reactivity.

Most   *3 1 2 5 4*   **Least**

1

1 mark

(c) Which of these metals could be lithium?

......*2*.........

0

1 mark

(d) Suggest one way the investigation could be improved to show which of these metals is the most reactive.

time how long it takes for a reaction to take place

0

1 mark

maximum 4 marks

5.   The diagram below shows the apparatus used
      to obtain pure water from impure water.

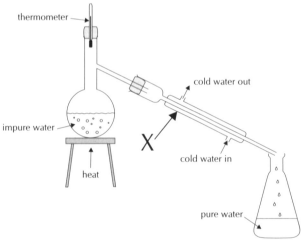

(a)   What is the name of this
       process of purifying water? ...*distallation*...

1 mark |1|

(b)   If you were to carry out this process, what
       temperature would the thermometer show?   ...*100*.. °C

1 mark |1|

(c)   The diagram shows a piece of apparatus labelled **X**. What is its function?

       ......*To clean and condense the water*......

       ....

1 mark |2|

The following diagram shows
particles in three states: solid, liquid
and gas. The arrows (1, 2, 3 and 4)
represent changes of state.

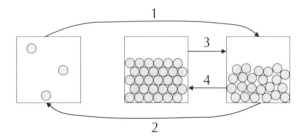

(d)   Write down the names of the four changes of
       state. Choose from the words in the box.

       1 ...*condensing*...   condensing   melting

       2 ...*boiling*...   bubbling   boiling

       3 ...*melting*...   filtering

       4 ...*freezing*...   freezing
                                  evaporating

4 marks |4|

(e)   Give the number (1, 2, 3 or 4) for the change of state which occurs in
       the following places in the apparatus from parts (a), (b) and (c).

            in piece of apparatus labelled X ...*1*...

            in the flask containing impure water ...*2*...

1 mark |1|

maximum 8 marks

6. (a) On the right is a picture showing a ray of blue light passing through a glass block.

ray of blue light

air

glass block

air

(i) When the light enters the glass block, it changes direction. Write the name of this effect.

.....*refraction*.........

| *1* |
1 mark

(ii) Most of the light goes into the glass block, but some of it doesn't go in. What happens to the light that **doesn't** go into the block?

.....*It gets absorbed by the block*.....

| *0* |
1 mark

(b) On the right is a picture showing white light going through a prism, and a spectrum forming on the white screen.

ray of white light

white screen

prism

spectrum

The spectrum includes light of all colours. Violet is at one end of the spectrum. On the right, write **blue**, **green** and **red** in the order of the spectrum.

.....*red*.....

.....*green*.....

.....*blue*.....

Violet

.....

| *1* |
1 mark

(c) Someone puts a red filter in the ray of white light. Tick the correct box to say what happens to the spectrum on the screen.

The whole spectrum disappears. ☐

The red part of the spectrum stays the same, but the other colours disappear. ☐

The red part of the spectrum disappears, but the other colours stay the same. ☑

The whole spectrum turns red. ☐

| *0* |
1 mark

maximum 4 marks

7. Research suggests that over half of the world's population uses biomass as a fuel for generating electricity.

(a) Explain what 'biomass' is.

....

....

☐ 1 mark

(b) Fossil fuels and biomass are both used as energy resources.
Write down the original source of this energy.

....

☐ 1 mark

(c) Name **three** fossil fuels which are often burned to generate electricity.

1. .... 2. ....

3. ....

☐ 2 marks

(d) Fossil fuels can be described as non-renewable energy resources.
Why are they called 'non-renewable'?

....

....

☐ 1 mark

(e) Some research indicates that there are many advantages
and disadvantages to burning different fuels.

(i) Write down **one** advantage of using fossil fuel
rather than biomass as an energy resource.

....

....

☐ 1 mark

(ii) Write down **one** advantage of using biomass rather
than fossil fuel as an energy resource.

....

....

☐ 1 mark

(iii) Write down **one disadvantage** of using both fossil
fuel and biomass as an energy resource.

....

....

☐ 1 mark

maximum 8 marks

8. The Earth is the third planet from the Sun.

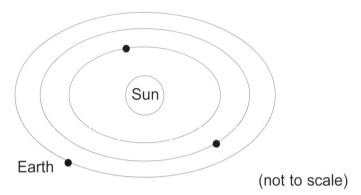

(not to scale)

(a) Name **one** planet closer to the Sun than Earth.

...... Mercury ....

d

1 mark

(b) A day and night on Jupiter lasts nearly 10 Earth hours.
Why is there daytime and night-time on Jupiter?

...... Jupiter spins around so that only
part gets sunlight ie daytime ....

1 mark

(c) Mars has summers and winters, like Earth.
Write down why there are seasons on Mars.

...... It is tilted on its axis too ....

....

1 mark

(d) Planets that are further from the Sun have longer years.
Explain why this is.

...... They have more to orbit around
the sun because they are far
away ....

2 marks

maximum 5 marks

9. In Britain, all children are able to have a vaccine against measles.
An injection makes them immune to the disease.

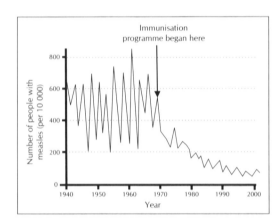

(a) What does the word 'immune' mean?

They won't be able to catch the disease

1 mark

(b) When a child is vaccinated, what do the white
blood cells produce to help kill micro-organisms?

antibodies

1 mark

(c) What is present in the vaccine to make white blood cells respond in this way?

chemicals

1 mark

(d) A new born baby is not vaccinated but it can have
immunity to measles for a short time. Explain why.

*It has only got enough white blood
cells to be immuned*

1 mark

(e) The programme of immunising children against measles was a success.
Describe how the graph shows this.

*the number of people with measles
decreased*

1 mark

(f) At present, an increasing number of people do **not** want to vaccinate
their children against measles. Write down what is likely to happen
to the number of people with measles as a result of this.

*The number of people would have
increased*

1 mark

maximum 6 marks

10. The picture shows a simple thermometer. Vicki made it using a capillary tube with a bulb and water dyed blue.

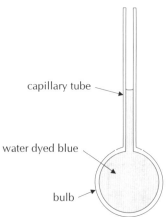

capillary tube

water dyed blue

bulb

(a) Vicki held the bulb in her hand. The bulb warmed up. Explain why the water rose up the capillary tube. Write your answer in terms of water molecules.

When water molecules are heated the particles vibrates causing it to push itself up the capillary tube

1 mark

1

(b) She tried to measure the temperature in a freezer by leaving the thermometer in it overnight. In the morning, the bulb of the thermometer had broken. Write down why this happened.

The water had frozen and expanded

1 mark

1

(c) Vicki made a new thermometer exactly like the first one. She wants to measure the temperature of hot syrup which will be over 115 °C. Will the thermometer be able to measure this? Explain your answer.

No, 115°C is too high

1 mark

0

(d) Vicki put the thermometer into hot water (around 70 °C). Initially, it had been at room temperature. She watched the water level. It dropped slightly before rising up the tube. Why did this happen? Circle the correct answer.

Volume of the bulb decreased before the water expanded.

Volume of the bulb increased before the water expanded.

Volume of water decreased before the water expanded.

Volume of the bulb decreased before the glass expanded.

1 mark

0

maximum 4 marks

11. A chicken gets energy from its food.
This picture shows what most of the energy is used for in a day.

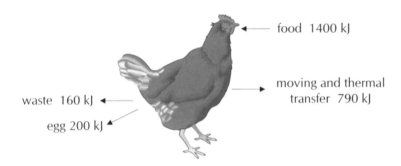

food 1400 kJ

moving and thermal
transfer 790 kJ

waste 160 kJ

egg 200 kJ

(a) Calculate the amount of energy that stays in the body of the chicken.

160 + 200 = 360 + 790 = 1150

1400 + 1150   2550 kJ

⬜ 0

1 mark

(b) What is this remaining energy used for?

to rest

⬜ 0

1 mark

(c) Energy from food is released by respiration in the cells of the chicken's body.
Complete this equation (in words) to show the process.

glucose + ...oxygen... → ...water... + ...energy...

⬜ 1

2 marks

(d) Write down **one** way in which a farmer could reduce the amount
of energy chickens lose by thermal transfer every day.

Don't let them out for so long

⬜ 1

1 mark

(e) A farmer can reduce the amount of energy transferred by moving and thermal
transfer from chickens. Write down **two** reasons why this is cost-efficient.

1. ....

....

2. ....

....

⬜

2 marks

12. This picture shows a bottle of tablets.

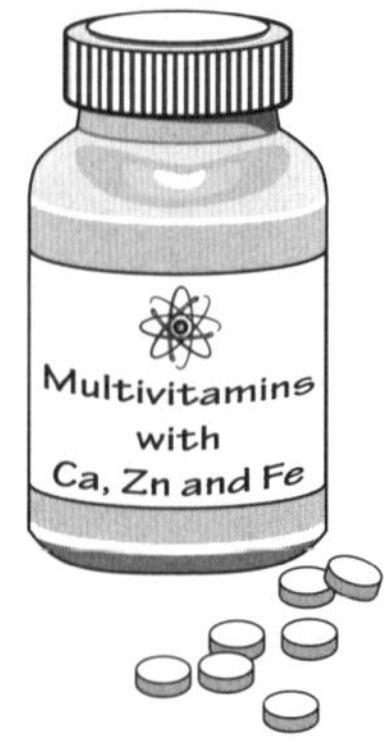

(a) To keep healthy, some people take tablets containing vitamins and minerals. Why would they want to take a tablet every day rather than a one-off dose?

....

....

....

The diagram below shows part of the Periodic Table. The three elements Ca, Zn and Fe written on the tablet bottle are shown in the table.

Li	Be										
Na	Mg										
K	Ca	Sc	Ti	V	Cr	Mn	Fe	Co	Ni	Cu	Zn
Rb	Sr	Y	Zr	Nb	Mo	Tc	Ru	Rh	Pd	Ag	Cd

(b) Element Ca is calcium. Write down the names of these other two elements.

Zn ...*Zinc*............   Fe .....*Iron*............

☐ *2*

2 marks

(c) Write down the symbol of the most reactive metal shown in the table above.

.......*Mg*..............

☐ *0*

1 mark

maximum 4 marks

13(a) A copper wire is coiled around a piece of plastic tube.
The wire is connected to a battery.
Three compasses are placed around the tube as shown in the diagram.

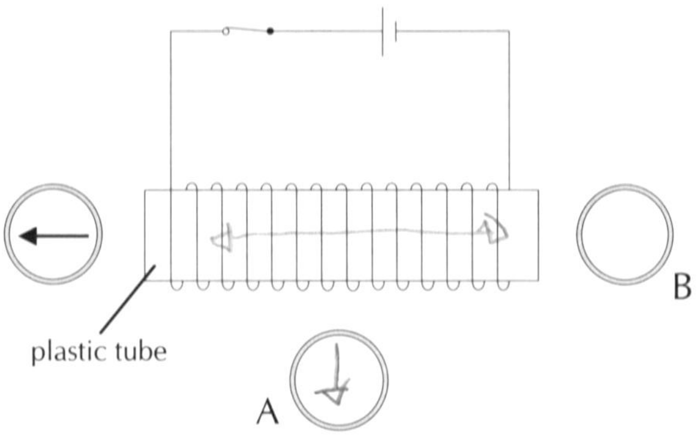

plastic tube

A   B

(i)   Draw arrows on compasses A and B to show the direction of
the magnetic field.

1 mark

(ii)   Draw an arrow in the middle of the plastic tube to show
the direction of the magnetic field inside the tube.

1 mark

(iii)   If the switch is opened, which direction
will all three compass needles point?   ......up...............

1 mark

(b)   Write down **one** way to reverse the direction of the magnetic field around the tube.

....

1 mark

....

(c)   Three small blocks of iron are then placed inside the tube.

(i)   The switch is closed. [The magnetic field stays the same as in part (a)]. The
iron becomes magnetised. Label all **six** poles on the blocks with either **N** or **S**.

1 mark

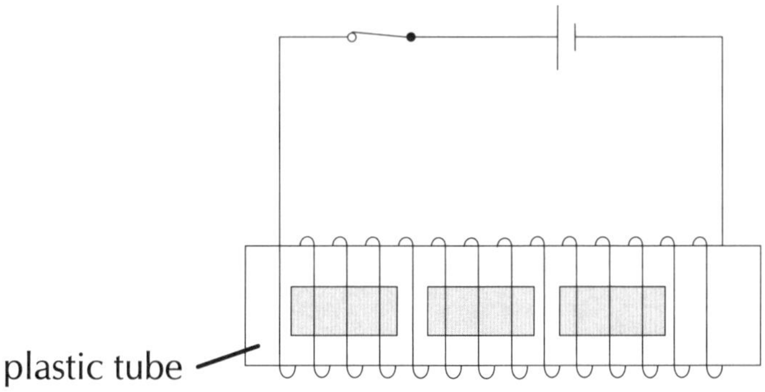

plastic tube

(ii)   The blocks of iron moved when the switch was closed. Why did they move?

1 mark

....

....

maximum 6 marks

© CGP 2002

14. This picture shows part of a human ear.
The ear drum vibrates when sound waves enter the ear.

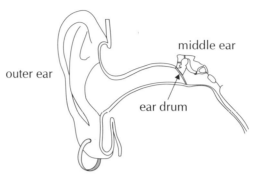

outer ear

middle ear

ear drum

A person is listening to a sound.

(a) If the pitch of the sound is increased, how
will the vibration of the ear drum change?

.....It will vibrate more quickly.....

| 1 |
1 mark

(b) If the sound is made louder, how will the vibration of the ear drum change?

.....It will vibrate louder.....

| 0 |
1 mark

(c) A person's ears can be damaged by loud sounds. Explain why.

.....ear drum has vibrated too much.....

| 0 |
1 mark

maximum 3 marks

Key Stage 3

Science Test

Practice Paper 2B

Read this page, but don't open the booklet until your teacher says you can start. Write your name and school in the spaces below.

First Name _anitta_

Last Name _____

School _____

Remember

- The test is one hour long.
- Make sure you have these things with you before you start: pen, pencil, rubber, ruler, angle measurer or protractor, calculator.
- The easier questions are at the start of the test.
- Try to answer all of the questions.
- Don't use any rough paper — write all your answers and working in this test paper.
- Check your work carefully before the end of the test.
- If you're not sure what to do, ask your teacher.

SCORE:			
	FIRST GO	SECOND GO	THIRD GO

1.   James rides a motorbike to work every day.
     Two horizontal forces affect its motion:
     forward force and **drag**.

drag ←   → forward force

(a)   Compare the sizes of the forward force and drag when:

(i)   The bike is speeding up.

The forward force is *decreasing and the*
drag increases

0

1 mark

(ii) The bike is moving at a steady 30 miles per hour.

The forward force is *equal to the Drag*

1

1 mark

(iii) The bike is slowing down.

The forward force is *increasing and*
the drag decreases

0

1 mark

(b)   (i)   Explain how molecules in the air cause **air resistance**.

The molecules hit the object that
is moving causing it to slow down

1

1 mark

(ii) Is air resistance larger or smaller when the bike is
      travelling faster? Explain your answer.

larger, because more air molecules
are hitting the object as it travels faster

2

2 marks

(c)   The forward force occurs because the tyres are **not** able to spin on the road.
      What force prevents them slipping?

friction

1

1 mark

maximum 7 marks

2. This diagram shows the planets in order out from the Sun.

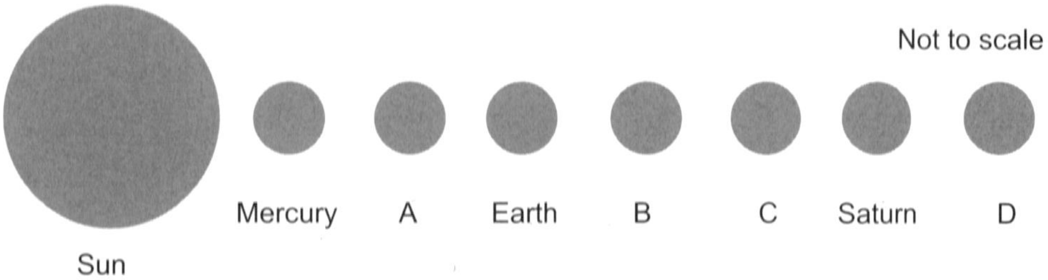

Not to scale

Sun   Mercury   A   Earth   B   C   Saturn   D

(a) What is the name of planet A? ...venus............................

`1`

1 mark

(b) Which planet is Mars? Circle the correct letter:

(B)   C   D

`1`

1 mark

(c) Which planet is Uranus? Circle the correct letter:

B   C   (D)

`1`

1 mark

(d) How long does it take the Earth to orbit around the Sun?

......365 ¼ days........

`1`

1 mark

(e) This table shows how long some other planets take to orbit the Sun.

Planet	Mercury	Mars	Saturn	Uranus
Time for one orbit of the Sun	88 days	687 days	29 years	84 years

All times are given in Earth days and years

Estimate how long it takes Venus to orbit the Sun.

......227 days......

`1`

1 mark

(f) A planet takes 12 Earth years to orbit the Sun.
Which planet is this?

......Jupiter......

`1`

1 mark

maximum 6 marks

3. Elaine's remote control car is controlled by two switches.
The circuit used to drive the motor is shown below.

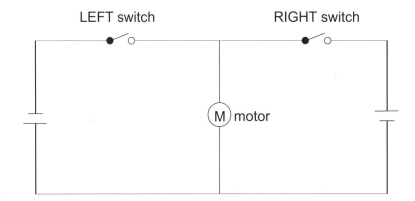

LEFT switch   RIGHT switch

M) motor

Look carefully at the way she has connected the two cells.
When she closes the left switch the motor turns.

(a) What, if anything, happens to the direction of the motor
if the left switch is open and the right switch closed?

The motor turns the opposite direction

1

1 mark

(b) Why should Elaine not close both switches at once?

It wouldn't work because the 2
electric current will fuse together

0

1 mark

(c) What would happen to the motor if she did?

It won't work

1

1 mark

(d)   She adds a resistor in the circuit.

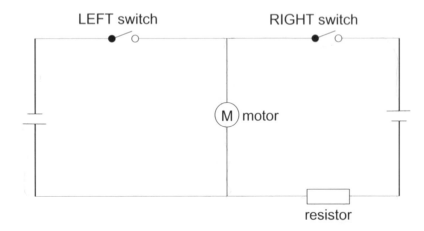

What difference does the resistor make to the motor:

(i)   when the left switch is closed and the right switch is open?

....

....

1 mark

(ii)   when the left switch is open and the right one closed?

....

....

1 mark

(e)   How could the original circuit be altered to give a two-speed motor that goes in one direction only?

....

....

1 mark

maximum 6 marks

4. A ray of **red** light falls on a glass prism as shown in the diagram.

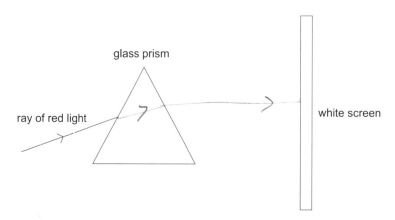

glass prism

ray of red light

white screen

(a) Using a ruler, draw on the diagram the path of the **red** ray through the prism to the screen.

2 marks

(b) The red ray is replaced by a ray of **white** light.

(i) What would you now see on the screen?

red light

 1

1 mark

A blue filter is placed between the prism and the screen.

(ii) What would you now see on the screen?

magenta

1 mark

(iii) Explain how the blue filter causes the change.

It absorbs with red to change colour

 1

1 mark

5. (a) Here are some processes which occur in the rock cycle:

1. Layers of mudstone are squeezed to form new minerals with flat crystals.
2. Grains of sediment collect in a layer on the sea bed.
3. Molten magma cools deep below the Earth's surface forming large crystals.
4. New crystals form in layers as rocks are affected by high temperature and increased pressure deep in the Earth's crust.
5. Grains of sediment are cemented together as they are buried deep under thick layers of other sediments.

(i) Which number represents a metamorphic process?

.................3...................

1 mark

(ii) Which number represents the formation of igneous rocks?

...................4....................

1 mark

(iii) Number 5 is an example of the formation of what type of rocks?

.........sedimentry........

1 mark

(iv) Which number could have led to the formation of granite?

.....................1.....................

1 mark

(b) Limestone is mainly calcium carbonate. It reacts with dilute hydrochloric acid to produce bubbles of gas.
Complete the word equation for the reaction.

Hydrochloric acid + calcium carbonate → water + calcium chloride + hydrogen carbonate

HCl + CaCO → H₂O

HCl CaC CO₂

2 marks

(c) Silicon dioxide is used to make glass for test tubes.
What, if anything, will happen when dilute hydrochloric acid is added to silicon dioxide?

.....a chemical reaction takesplace....................

1 mark

maximum 7 marks

6. Chris is given seven different liquids and tests their pH.

liquid number	1	2	3	4	5	6	7
pH of liquid	4.0	8.5	3.5	2.0	13.0	7	2.5

(a) Which of the following could have been used by Chris to obtain the result? **Tick the correct box(es)**.

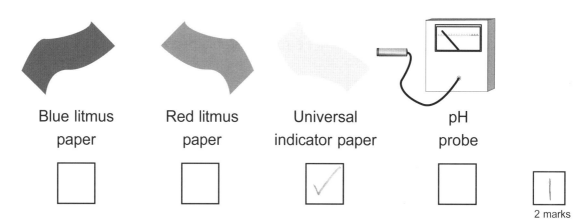

Blue litmus paper	Red litmus paper	Universal indicator paper	pH probe
☐	☐	✓	☐

2 marks

(b) Give one thing Chris could do to ensure that his results were as accurate as possible.

......Repeat the tests again............

1 mark

(c) Which liquid is the weakest acid?

............1............

1 mark

(d) What kind of reaction occurs if liquid 2 is added to liquid 3?

......neutralisation......

1 mark

(e) Which liquid is most likely to be sodium hydroxide solution?

............4............

1 mark

maximum 6 marks

7. (a) Copper carbonate is heated in a crucible.

The reaction taking place is

copper carbonate ➔ copper oxide + carbon dioxide

The crucible and its contents are weighed before and after.

Item	Mass/g
empty crucible	25
crucible and copper carbonate	27.32
crucible and copper oxide	26.29

What mass of carbon dioxide is given off by the reaction? Give the unit.

.... 2.32 g ....

0

1 mark

(b) Magnesium is then heated in a crucible.
Again the masses are recorded before and after.

Item	Mass/g
empty crucible	25
crucible and magnesium	25.24
crucible and magnesium oxide	26.32

(i) Give the word equation for the reaction taking place this time.

... magnesium ➔ magnesium oxide + methane

0

1 mark

(ii) Explain why the mass increases this time.

... methane is given of

0

1 mark

maximum 3 marks

© CGP 2002

8. (a) The graph below shows how the length of a human foetus increases during the first 30 weeks of pregnancy.

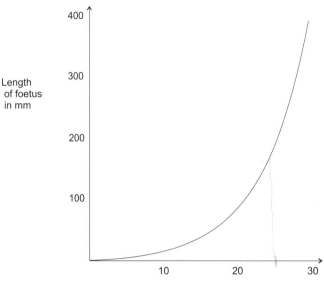

Age of foetus in weeks

In which 5 week period on the graph does the mass of the foetus increase most rapidly?

.... 20 - 25 ....

(b) In the womb, the foetus is surrounded by a liquid called amniotic fluid. Give **one** function of the amniotic fluid.

......Protects the foetus...................................

....

(c) The foetus needs oxygen but cannot breathe while it's in the uterus. Explain how oxygen gets from the **air** into the cells of the **foetus**.

......Air is given by the unbilical card......

......and placenta onto the cells of......

......the foetus......

....

maximum 6 marks

9. The diagram shows a rectangular coil attached to 2 batteries by wires.
The coil is wrapped around a **plastic** tube. It has two **steel** rods in.
The rods are lying parallel and touching but are free to move.

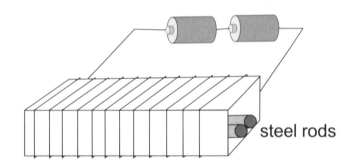

steel rods

(a) When the batteries are attached, the rods move apart.

   (i) Explain why this happens.

   A magnetic feild is produced
   when the batteries touch
   causing the steel rods to repel

 2

2 marks

   (ii) What happens when the batteries are disconnected?

   The magnetic feild is not
   present and the steel rods are
   free to move, attract

 0

1 mark

(b) One of the rods is replaced with a wooden stick.

   Explain what will happen this time:

   Ther rods will move but the
   wooden stick won't

2 marks

maximum 5 marks

10. Monsieur Velo cycles around France selling onions.

A cardboard sheet gets stuck to the frame of his bike.

As the wheel turns, the spokes hit the card and a 'musical' tone is made.

(a) Explain why the **card** makes a 'musical' tone.

It vibrates

1 mark

(b) What happens to the pitch of the note as he cycles faster?

It becomes higher, increases

1 mark

(c) Monsieur Velo notices that the card is making the wheel slow down.

(i) Describe the energy change which is happening as the wheel slows down.

The bike slows down de⋯

0

1 mark

(ii) What will happen to the pitch of the 'musical' tone as the wheel slows down?

It will slow down

0

1 mark

maximum 4 marks

11. Look at this section of the periodic table.

				H					Non metals

metals

								He
Li	Be	B	C	N	O	F	Ne
Na	Mg	Al	Si	P	S	Cl	Ar

(a) Mark on the table metals and non-metals.

0

1 mark

(b) What are the symbols for

(i) magnesium   *mg*

(ii) carbon   *C*

2

2 marks

(c) What are the chemical names of these compounds:

(i) NaCl   *Sodium Chloride*

(iii) MgS   *Magnesium sulphide*

2

2 marks

(d) What is the common name for NaCl?   ....

1 mark

(e) Name, from the table, **one** element which is a gas at room temperature and has atoms which are joined in molecules.

   Helium

1 mark

(f) What is the most reactive metal shown in the table above?

   Sodium

1

1 mark

maximum 8 marks

12. John uses his empty king-size peanut butter jar to make a garden.
He keeps it in a brightly lit room with the sealed lid on.

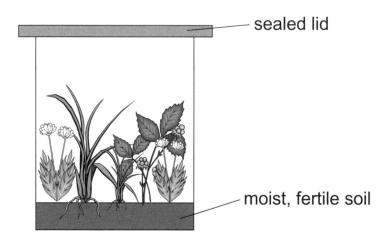

sealed lid

moist, fertile soil

(a) Complete the following sentences to explain what happens to the carbon dioxide and oxygen levels in the jar over a week.

(i) The plants use carbon dioxide in the process of:

.... *Photosynthesis* ....

1 mark

(ii) This process produces:

.... *oxygen / glucose* ....

1 mark

(iii) The gas produced by the bacteria in the soil is:

.... *oxygen* ....

1 mark

(iv) This process is called:

.... *respiration* ....

1 mark

(b)   Plants cross-pollinate by transferring pollen from one plant to another.
Give two reasons why this is more likely to happen in a normal
outdoor garden than in the bottled garden.

1. There is wind and bees

2.

2 marks

(c)   The plants need the bacteria in the soil because they break up the dead parts
of plants. They also release nitrates which are a source of nitrogen for the plant.

Why does the plant need nitrogen to grow?

For Strong plant growth

1 mark

(d)   Apart from nitrogen, there are two other minerals that plants need in large quantities.
Name one of them.

phosphate , potassium

1 mark

maximum 8 marks

13. A research biologist investigated four different habitats and produced the four pyramids of numbers below.

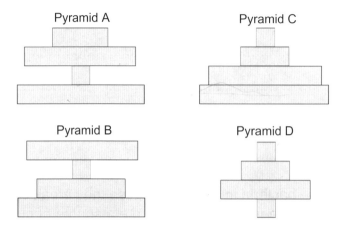

Pyramid A

Pyramid C

Pyramid B

Pyramid D

Her observations are given below.
Match the observation to the correct pyramid of numbers.

(a) **Observation**

- Buffalos eat grass.
- Ticks live on buffalos and suck their blood.
- Birds eat ticks.

This matches pyramid ....B.......

1 mark

(b) **Observation**

- Minnows eat waterweed.
- Perch eat minnows.
- Pikes eat perch.

This matches pyramid ......A.......

1 mark

(c) **Observation**

- Wild pigs eat fruit.
- Jaguars eat wild pigs.
- Fleas live on jaguars and drink their blood.

This matches pyramid ......D.......

1 mark

(d) **Observation**

- Oak trees provide food for caterpillars.
- Robins eat caterpillars.
- Cats eat robins.

This matches pyramid ......C.......

1 mark

maximum 4 marks

SHP3U

10w L6.
39

Key Stage 3

Science Test

Practice Paper 3A

Read this page, but don't open the booklet until your teacher says you can start. Write your name and school in the spaces below.

First Name _anitta_

Last Name _Sharma_

School _____

Remember

- The test is one hour long.
- Make sure you have these things with you before you start: pen, pencil, rubber, ruler, angle measurer or protractor, calculator.
- The easier questions are at the start of the test.
- Try to answer all of the questions.
- Don't use any rough paper — write all your answers and working in this test paper.
- Check your work carefully before the end of the test.
- If you're not sure what to do, ask your teacher.

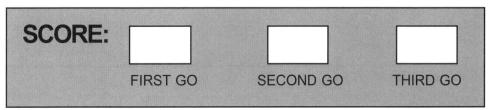

SCORE:			
	FIRST GO	SECOND GO	THIRD GO

Exam Set SHP31

© CGP 2002

1. The pictures below show plant and animal cells with different functions.

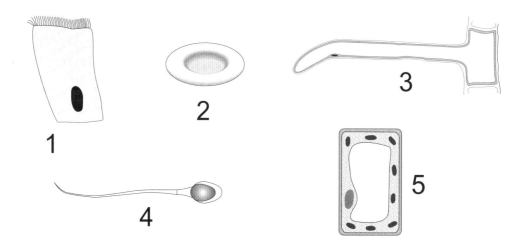

(a) Write down the name of cell 2.

red blood cell

(b) Two of the cells have the functions listed below.
Write down the correct cell number next to the function.

    (i)   movement of mucus   *1*

    (ii)   photosynthesis   *5*

(c) Write down the name of the organ where cell 4 is produced.

testis

(d) Write down the name of the part of the plant where cell 3 is found.

the roots

maximum 5 marks

2. A gardener grew radish plants on her allotment. She dug up all the radishes at the same time. The pictures below show two of the radish plants.

radish plant 1   radish plant 2

(a) Plant 1 came from a part of the allotment that was kept free of weeds.
Plant 2 came from a part of the allotment that was covered with weeds.

Write down **two** ways in which the weeds may have stopped plant 2 growing as healthy and as big as plant 1.

1. .....*taken up space for growth*.....✓.............

....

2. .....*taken most of light for*...................

.....*photosynthesis*.........✗ ✓ *took*.............

available water

/

2 marks

(b) Write down why the gardener's plants would produce larger roots when they received more light.

.....*The leaves of the plant would*.....
.....*be able to photosynthesis ✓ which*.....
.....*would produce glucose a food*✗.....
.....*for the plant* ✓.....
.....*— transported to or stored*.....
.....*in roots*.....

2

3 marks

maximum 5 marks

© CGP 2002

3. The notes below are taken from a scientist's note pad.
She has been doing field work in a snakes habitat.

> Date: 12 December 2002
> Location: West Africa
>
> Weather: Dry and hot
> Temperature: 40°C
> Time: 12:00 noon
> The Royal Python snakes have
> all returned to their holes or
> are sheltering under rocks.
>
> page 1

(a) Write down **two** ways that staying in a hole
in the ground could help a snake to survive.

1. *They won't get too hot* ✓

2. *Easier to catch their prey* ✓

2

2 marks

> Date : 12 December 2002
> Location: West Africa
> Royal Python observed
> wrapping its body around a
> small mammal – squeezed
> until it died.
> Did not bite prey as it has
> no venom.
>
> page 2

(b) Write down **two** ways in which this could kill the prey.

1. *squeeze mammal until dead* ✓

2. *Use poisonous venom to kill
prey* ✗ *damages or crushes
organs*

1

2 marks

maximum 4 marks

4.   (a)   Below is a paragraph describing the menstrual cycle.
Fill in the gaps by choosing words from the list.

the middle	**weekly cycle**	**the uterus**
an ovary	**the start**	**the end**
yearly cycle	**the vagina**	**monthly cycle**

Menstruation is the first part of a ....._monthly_ _cycle_.

The cycle starts when the lining of ....._the_ _uterus_.......... breaks down.

An ovum (egg) is released from ...._the_ _ovary_....... at roughly

....._the_ _middle_. of each cycle.

[4]

4 marks

(b)   When adolescent, a boy's body changes.
Describe **two** of the changes that take place.

....._Voice_ _deepens_ _and_ _hair_ _start_ _to_......

....._grow_ _on_ _face_.....................................

....

....

[2]

2 marks

(c)   The changes that take place during the menstrual cycle and at
adolescence are controlled by chemicals released by glands in the body.
What is the general name for those chemicals?

....._hormones_..

[1]

1 mark

maximum 7 marks

© CGP 2002

5. An igneous rock, for example granite, can become a sedimentary rock.
A model of the process was carried out in a school laboratory as shown below.

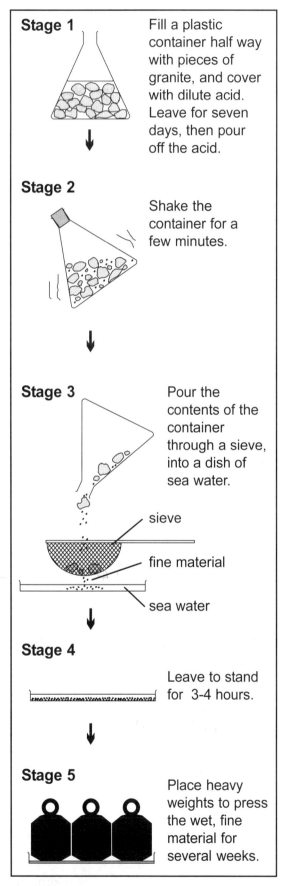

Stage 1 Fill a plastic container half way with pieces of granite, and cover with dilute acid. Leave for seven days, then pour off the acid.

Stage 2 Shake the container for a few minutes.

Stage 3 Pour the contents of the container through a sieve, into a dish of sea water.

sieve

fine material

sea water

Stage 4 Leave to stand for 3-4 hours.

Stage 5 Place heavy weights to press the wet, fine material for several weeks.

(a) Chemical weathering in the rock cycle is shown in Stage 1. Which part of the rock cycle does Stage 2 show?

the eroding away of rocks

| 1 |

1 mark

(b) Pieces of granite are carried from a mountain to the sea. The pieces of granite change as they are carried. Describe **two** ways they change.

They break into pieces and change shape &
• smoothed and rounded
• get smaller

| 0 |

2 marks

(c) Stages 4 and 5 represent parts of the rock cycle. Which **two** parts do they represent?

Stage 4:

a layer of sediment &

Deposition

| 0 |

1 mark

Stage 5:

Compressed sediment for years /

| 0 |

1 mark

Compression

maximum 5 marks

6. This graph shows the solubility of two salts in water at different temperatures.
Solubility is the mass (in grams) of salt which will dissolve in 100 g of water.

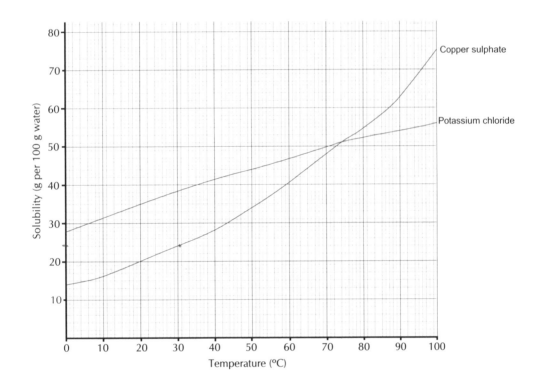

(a) Using the graph, describe how the solubility of
copper sulphate changes with temperature.

The higher the temperature, the more copper sulphate dissolved

| 1 |
1 mark

(b) Use the graph to answer these questions:

(i) At what temperature are the solubilities of both salts the same? ...74..... °C

| 1 |
1 mark

(ii) What is the solubility of copper sulphate at 30 °C? ...24..... g per 100 g water

| |
1 mark

(c) Solubility of salts in water is normally given for temperatures between
0 °C and 100 °C. Why is it only given for this range of temperatures?

Above 100° water would boil and evaporate to become a gas & water freezes at 0°C

| 1 |
2 marks

maximum 5 marks

7. A boy throws a brick into an **empty** swimming pool.
He can't see the brick from where he's standing.

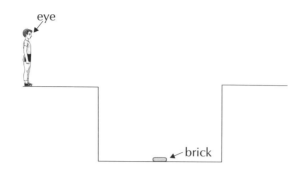

The swimming pool is filled with water. The boy stands in
the same position but now he can see part of the brick.

(a) Using a ruler, draw a ray of light on the diagram **below** to show how the boy
sees part of the brick. Put an arrow on the ray to show the direction.

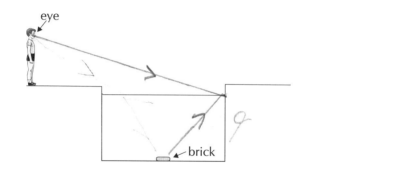

3 marks

(b) What is the name of the process that allows the boy to see the brick?

.........reflection..........& refraction...........

1 mark

(c) The boy poured blue food dye into the pool. The dye acts like a blue
filter and the brick now looks blue. Explain how a blue filter works.

......The blue filter works as all.........
....the other colours get absorbed.......
...apart from blue.........................

2 marks

maximum 6 marks

8. This diagram shows the orbit of the Earth around the Sun.

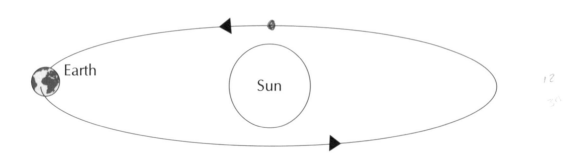

(a) Write down the name of **one** planet which is closer to the Sun than the Earth.

mercury

1 mark

(b) Write down the name of **one** planet which is further from the Sun than the Earth.

pluto

1 mark

(c) In the daytime, Britain is in the sunlight. At night, Britain is in the Earth's dark shadow. Explain why we have both day and night.

As the earth spins only one side recieves light (daytime) and the other dark (night).

1 mark

(d) On the diagram above, **draw** the Earth nine months later than where it is shown. **Explain** (in the space below) why you chose this position.

Divide 360° by 12 months and you get 3 months. 12 ÷ 3 = 4 sections
9

0

1 mark

take 1 year to go around sun . 9 months is 3/4 — 3/4 around

maximum 4 marks

© CGP 2002

9. Some airport runways are made of concrete. It is laid down in sections with small gaps in between.

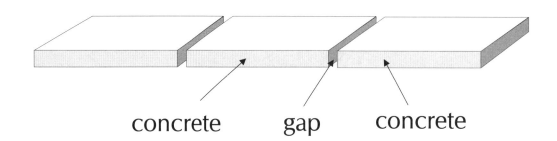

concrete   gap   concrete

(a) What happens to the **size** of most objects when they heat up?

They contract & expand

1 mark

(b) As temperature rises, what happens to the gaps between the concrete sections?

They become bigger & shrink

1 mark

(c) What might happen to the sections of concrete if the temperature rises and there are **no** gaps between them?

— cracks, slip over each othe

1 mark

(d) The constructors fill the gaps between the concrete sections with **tar**. The tar becomes soft when it is warm. Why is the tar's softness important?

— squished, allowing concrete to expand

1 mark

maximum 4 marks

10. Four year nine students studied a local woodland and produced this diagram of a woodland food web.

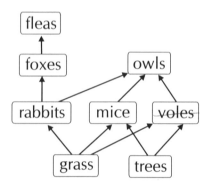

(a) During their fieldwork, a disease killed all the voles in the woodland.

One student predicted that this would make the population of mice go up, while another student predicted that this would make the population of mice go down. Write down reasons why the population of mice could go up or go down.

up .....*There would be more grass and* .....

.....*trees to feed on* .....

1 mark

down .....*more get eaten by owls.* .....

1 mark

(b) Draw a **pyramid of numbers** in the space below for this food chain:

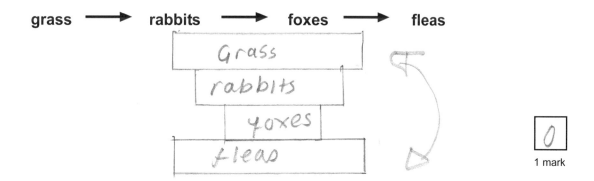

grass → rabbits → foxes → fleas

Grass
rabbits
foxes
fleas

0

1 mark

maximum 3 marks

11. A student doctor removed some of the fluid from a person's stomach. The fluid was put into a tube. Pieces of cooked ham were added. The diagram shows the tube during the experiment. The ham had completely digested after 6 hours.

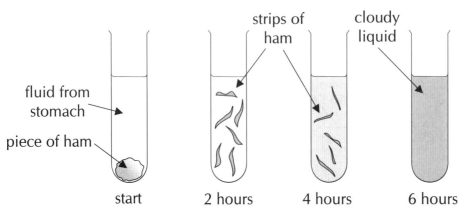

(a) (i) Name a substance in the fluid from the stomach that caused the ham to be digested after 6 hours.

..Hydrochloric acid & an enzyme..

☉ 1 mark

(ii) Why did the student doctor keep the tube at 37 °C?

...so that the acid wouldn't boile — temp that enzymes work best at

◑ 1 mark

(b) The digestion of protein starts in the stomach and finishes in the small intestine.

(i) Name something that the digested protein is used for in the body.

...repair damaged areas...

| 1 mark

(ii) How do the products of digestion move from the small intestine to cells in the rest of the body?

...They diffuse into the cells by the cappilaries which then take it to the rest of the body 2 — pass through intestines wall carried by blood vessels

◑ 2 marks

(c) The stomach fluid contains a strong acid. Apart from any role this might have in digestion, what does this acid do?

..It gives the food a right ph and breaks it down into smaller molecules & ⇒ kill microbes

◑ 1 mark

maximum 6 marks

12. Matt uses a pump to inflate a balloon.
He notices that the pump gets hot as he uses it.

(a) How and where was the energy stored before it was transferred to pump up the balloon?

......Chemical.....energy.....................................

0

2 marks

(b) Explain how the gas molecules inside the balloon exert pressure on the walls of the balloon.

......They..get...lots..of..energy...and...collide.....

.....against..the...walls..of..the...balloon.

1

1 mark

(c) The air going into the balloon is warmed up by the pumping.
How will this affect the motion of the gas molecules inside the balloon?

......They'll...collide..and..speed..up.

1

1 mark

(d) As the air in the balloon becomes hotter, the pressure rises. Write down **one** reason, in terms of the motion of gas molecules, why the pressure rises.

—......more.......collisions...with...balloon

0

1 mark

(e) As Matt pumps more air into the balloon, the pressure inside it increases. Explain why the greater number of gas molecules increases pressure in the balloon.

—......more..collisions...with..balloon..........

0

1 mark

maximum 6 marks

13. This table shows what happens when four elements (1, 2, 3 and 4) are burned in air, added to water or added to dilute hydrochloric acid.

Element	1	2	3	4
heated in air	slow – forms basic oxide	burns – forms basic oxide	burns – forms acidic oxide	burns – forms basic oxide
water	none	vigorous – gives off hydrogen	none	none
dilute hydrochloric acid	none	violent – gives off a gas	none	vigorous – gives off a gas

(a) Elements 1, 2 and 4 are all metals. Write down the numbers of the metals in order of reactivity. Start with the **most** reactive.

......2......   ......4......   ....3..1....

0

1 mark

(b) One gas, present in air, reacts with all four elements.
Write down the name of the gas.

......oxygen......

1

1 mark

(c) Element 4 gives off a gas when it reacts with hydrochloric acid.
Write down the name of the gas.

......hydrogen......

1

1 mark

(d) Using the information in the table, how can you tell that element 3 is the only non–metal?

......It reacts with water and......
......gives of gas & — forms acidic oxide

0

1 mark

(e) Write down **one** name of an element that could be element 2.

...hydrochloric acid
& sodium

0

1 mark

maximum 5 marks

14. The picture shows a person ringing a church bell.

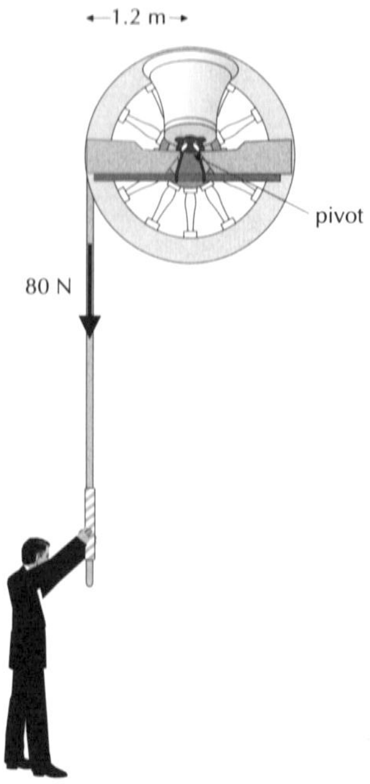

←1.2 m→

pivot

80 N

The bell is attached upside down to a wheel
of radius 1.2 m.
To ring the bell, the rope is pulled.

(a) The bell-ringer pulls on the rope with a downward
force of 80 N. Calculate the moment (turning
effect) on the wheel. Write down the unit.

80 N × 1.2 m = 96 N/M

2

2 marks

(b) The wheel turns as the rope is pulled. When it is travelling at its highest speed,
the rope moves 0.6 m in 0.05 s. Find the speed. Write down the unit.

0.6 ÷ 0.05 = 12 ÷ 10

1.2 m/s

0

2 marks

(c) The bell is rung twice. The second ring is quieter.
Both rings have identical pitch.
Complete the sentences below by filling in the blanks.

2

2 marks

The frequency of the second	The amplitude of the second
ring was _equal to_	ring was _smaller then_
the frequency of the first ring.	the amplitude of the first ring.

(d) Most people can hear the sound of a bell.
Circle the most likely frequency of a bell ringing.

300 Hz

3 Hz

30 000 Hz

3 000 000 Hz

0

1 mark

(e) Energy is given out when the bell rings. This energy was originally stored in
the bell-ringer's body. Describe the sequence of the main energy transfers
involved when a person rings a church bell.

– chemical/potential energy in bell
ringer, as bell swings kinetic
energy changes into potential energy
becomes sound energy

0

3 marks

maximum 10 marks

Blank Page

SHP3U

Key Stage 3

Science Test

Practice Paper 3B

Read this page, but don't open the booklet until your teacher says you can start. Write your name and school in the spaces below.

First Name _anita_

Last Name _Sharma_

School

Remember

- The test is one hour long.
- Make sure you have these things with you before you start: pen, pencil, rubber, ruler, angle measurer or protractor, calculator.
- The easier questions are at the start of the test.
- Try to answer all of the questions.
- Don't use any rough paper — write all your answers and working in this test paper.
- Check your work carefully before the end of the test.
- If you're not sure what to do, ask your teacher.

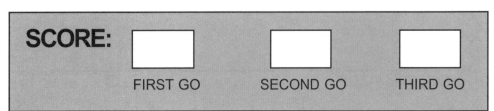

SCORE:			
	FIRST GO	SECOND GO	THIRD GO

© CGP 2002

1. Richard is doing an experiment about how easily a brick slides along a rough wooden table.

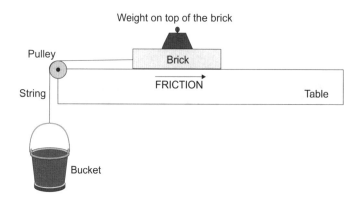

(a)   He does the experiment with different weights on the brick and counts how many 1kg bags of sugar he has to put in the bucket to make the brick slide. His results are in the table.

Weight on the brick (N)	0	1	2	3	4
Number of bags of sugar needed	1	3	5	7	9

(i)   Describe how the number of bags of sugar needed in the bucket varies with the weight on top of the brick.

The more weight on the brick the bags of sugar needed

1 mark

(ii)   Richard puts a 4.5 N weight on the brick. How many bags of sugar would he need to make it slide?

10 bags

1 mark

(b)　He tries the experiment again on a shiny varnished table.

(i)　How will the results change on the new table?

a more numbery of sugar neededa — fewer bags

0

1 mark

(ii)　Suggest another way, with the same table, brick and weight that Richard could reduce the friction.

slant the table & add lubricant such as oil

0

1 mark

maximum 4 marks

© CGP 2002

2. You can see satellites in the sky at night.
They look like stars moving across the sky.

(a) Stars produce their own light but satellites do not.
Explain how you can see satellites.

light is reflected to the satellites onto our eyes by the sun

2

2 marks

(b) Satellites sometimes become invisible for periods of the night and then reappear later in a different part of the sky.
Explain what is happening.

The earth is spinning on its axis, so the satellite will appear somewhere else, and only part of the earth recieves light
— earth moves between sun & satellites

0

1 mark

(c) What are satellites orbiting the Earth used for? Give **one** example.

Communication

1

1 mark

maximum 4 marks

3. Look at this circuit diagram.

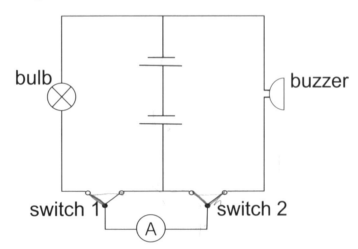

bulb

buzzer

switch 1

switch 2

A

Complete the table showing what happens with the
switches in different positions:

Switch 1	Switch 2	Is the bulb lit?	Does the buzzer sound?	Ammeter reading +ve, -ve or zero
Right	Right	No	Yes	-ve
Right	Left	No	Yes	+ ve
Left	Right	yes	No	+ ve
Left	Left	yes	Yes	zero

understood

5 marks

maximum 5 marks

4. (a) Observations show that the Arctic Hare changes its coat in the summer and winter.

In summer   In winter

Give **two** ways in which growing a white furry coat in the winter helps the arctic hare survive.

1 ..... *keep itself warm* ....

....

2 ..... *Camoflage itself with snow, to* .....
..... *stop getting eaten.* ....

3

3 marks

(b) Animals get characteristics from their parents.
Complete the following sentences:

(i) Information about an animal's characteristics is passed on in a molecule called ..... *DNA* ..... .

|

1 mark

(ii) The female's genes are passed on in the egg.

The male's genes are passed on in the ..... *sperm* ..... .

|

1 mark

(iii) The genes are held in the ..... *nucleus* ..... of the cells.

|

1 mark

(iv) The process of passing characteristics by genes has a special name.

We say the children ..... *have* ..... characteristics

from their parents.   ✗

           inherit

0

1 mark

maximum 7 marks

5. Chocosnaps breakfast cereal claims to have 'added iron'.

(a) Lyndsay decides to test if the cereal contains tiny pieces of powdered iron metal. Here is her experiment:

> I crushed 100g of chocosnaps into a fine powder and mixed it with water. Then I put a white, plastic coated magnet into the mixture and stirred.

If the chocosnaps contain pieces of iron metal, what will happen?

It would become magnetised.
- iron will be attached to magnet

0

1 mark

(b) Give two differences between iron metal and compounds containing iron.

1 _iron metal is an element._ ✓

2 _Its just iron, it doesn't contain anything else_ of _iron compound aren't magnetic_

1

2 marks

(c) In Lyndsay's stomach, hydrochloric acid helps break up the food. Complete the reaction of hydrochloric acid and iron.

iron + hydrochloric acid ➔ _hydrogen_ + _iron chloride_
Fe   HCl

2

2 marks

(d) Iron is used by the body to make red blood cells which transport oxygen around the body.
People who are anaemic do not have enough red blood cells. Why would they feel like they don't have much energy?

Because they haven't got enough iron and their cells arn't recieving enough oxygen - need oxyged to produce energy

1

2 marks

maximum 7 marks

6. Keith wants to find out which snack has the highest energy content.
He does an experiment to look at the amount of energy in two brands of crisps.

He burns a sample of the food to see how much this raises the temperature
of the water in the test tube. This rise in temperature uses energy from the food.

(a) Suggest two things Keith should have done to make the experiment a fair test:

1....repeat..the..test@...same..amount..of..water

2.....same...amount...of...food...from...each

1

2 marks

(b) Keith should also take some precautions to increase the safety of the
experiment. Give **two** things he could do to make the experiment safer.

1....Worn..goggles..........................

2......wear...gloves..of..point...test..tube...
.............................away..from..hym

1

2 marks

(c) The table shows nutritional details from the packets of the different brands.

	energy in kJ	protein in g	carbohydrate in g	fat in g	fibre in g
100 g of Runners' plain crisps	2050	6.2	56.2	28.7	4.2
100 g of Henry's Health Snack	1300	9.2	45.1	10.5	9.1

He repeats his experiment using 10 grams of each brand.

Write down the letter of the correct statement.

A: The temperature will rise more with the Runners' Crisps.

B: The temperature change will be the same.

C: The temperature will rise more with the Henry's Health snack.

The correct statement is statement ...A....

1

1 mark

(d) (i) Explain why the energy in fibre can **not** be used by the human body.

There isn't enough ~~g~~

— fibre is not digested

0

1 mark

(ii) Why is fibre an important part of a balanced diet?

It keep the digestive system

fit and healthy (working)

1

1 mark

(iii) Using the table, give **two** reasons why Henry's Health Snacks are healthier than Runners' plain crisps.

• less fat

• more protien

2

2 marks

(e) Neither snack contains vitamin C. Give an example of a type of food which provides a good source of vitamin C.

orange

1

1 mark

maximum 10 marks

7. The diagram shows a sketch of a cell from a rabbit as seen down a powerful microscope.

(a) Label the diagram:

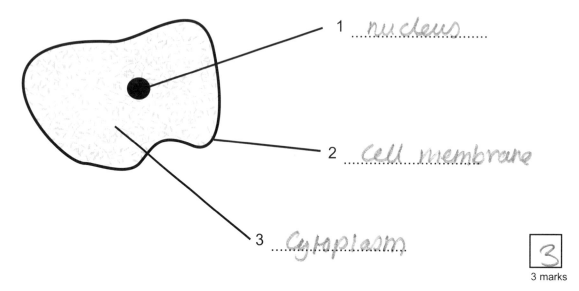

1 *nucleus*

2 *cell membrane*

3 *Cytoplasm*

3

3 marks

(b) Name two parts which would be found in a plant cell and not in an animal one.

1 *cell wall*

2 *vacuole*

2

2 marks

(c) The cell is one of a group of similar cells working together. What is such a group of similar cells called?

a tissue

1

1 mark

maximum 6 marks

8. Denise is running along the street past some lamp posts.

The lamp posts are equally spaced at 10 metres apart.

Anna starts timing Denise at the first lamp post and takes a photo of her running 10 seconds later.

1st lamp post   After 10 seconds

(a)   (i)   How far has she travelled in those ten seconds? (Give the correct units)

40 metres, g 30 m   nd

0   1 mark

     (ii)   How fast is Denise running?

40 metres ÷ 10 second = 4

4   m/s

0   1 mark

9 3

(b)   Denise keeps running at the same speed.

From the time the photo is taken, it takes her a further 35 seconds to reach the bus stop. How much further has she run in this time?

35 × 4 = 140

140   m

0   1 mark

2   105

(c)   Anna's camera uses a flash to take the photo. How does the light from the flash get back to the camera to make the photograph?

It reflects back into the camera

1   1 mark

maximum 4 marks

9. Copper is extracted from an ore called copper pyrites.
The formula of copper pyrites is $CuFeS_2$.

(a) Beside copper, what are the other two elements in the compound?

1. ...... Iron ....

2. ...... Sulphur ....

| 1 |
1 mark

(b) Copper is obtained by heating the ore in a controlled supply of air with sand (SiO_2). The reaction is shown below:

$$2CuFeS_2 + 5O_2 + 2SiO_2 \rightarrow 2Cu + 4SO_2 + 2FeSiO_3$$

(i) If there is too much oxygen, what substance would be formed?

...... water vapour or copper oxide

| 0 |
1 mark

(ii) A factory uses this reaction. It removes the waste gas sulphur dioxide (SO_2). Explain why the sulphur dioxide should be removed.

...... It can be toxic and ......
...... poisonous or ......
− Acid rain ......
− Poisons aquatic organisms ......

| 0 |
2 marks

(iii) The sulphur dioxide is removed by bubbling it through a solution which reacts with it. What **type** of solution is used to remove the sulphur dioxide?

...... dilute hydrochloric acid or ......
...... alkaline

| 0 |
1 mark

(c) Copper is a very useful metal. State one of its uses, and give a property of copper that makes it good for this use.

Use: ...... transport water for heating ......
Property: ...... good heat insulator or ......
− cooking pots
− good conductor of heat

| 0 |
2 marks

maximum 7 marks

10. The diagram below shows an electromagnetic relay in a circuit with a switch, a lamp and a battery.

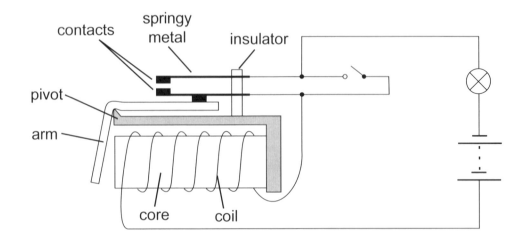

(a)   (i)   What would be a suitable material for the core of the electromagnet?

..................................Iron..................................

☐ 1

1 mark

(ii)   Name a suitable material to use for the arm resting on the pivot.

.........Copper   Iron or nickle, or.........
cobalt

☐ 0

1 mark

(b)   The two contacts come together when the switch is closed.
Explain why.

.....They attract.....
- Core becomes magnetised
- arm is attracted to core
- Pivot pushes contacts
      to gether

☐ 1

3 marks

(c)   Explain why the bulb stays lit when the switch is opened again.

.....It still has enough electricity.....

☐ 0

1 mark

maximum 6 marks

11. A candle burns under a glass jar.

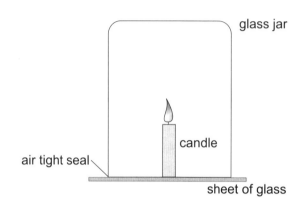

glass jar

candle

air tight seal

sheet of glass

(a) (i) There is a reaction when the candle burns.
Give the chemical formulae of **two** of the products of this reaction.

1. Carbon dioxide ✓

2. water vapour g) H₂O or CO or C

1

2 marks

(ii) What could you see to show that a chemical reaction
is taking place? Give **two** examples.

1. water vapour, with steam

2. candle melts & soot or heat given off

1

2 marks

(b) The candle is replaced with a pot plant.

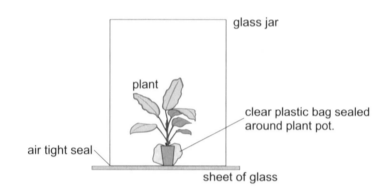

glass jar

plant

clear plastic bag sealed
around plant pot.

air tight seal

sheet of glass

(i) What effect does the plant's photosynthesis have on
the levels of different gases in the jar?

1. *It won't photosynthesis*

2. *respire instead*

- CO₂ levels decrease
+ O₂ levels rises

0

2 marks

(ii) If you covered the jar with a black bag, what effect
would this have on these changes?

*no light means no photosynthesis,
which means no food, it will
die / No Photosynthesis, respiration
continues*

0

2 marks

(c) Plants need chlorophyll to photosynthesise.

(i) Which part of the cell contains chlorophyll?

Chloroplast

1

1 mark

(ii) Which part of the cell controls chlorophyll production?

nucleus

1

1 mark

maximum 10 marks

© CGP 2002

12. On the remote Isle of Goff near Scotland, two new varieties of sheep are found.
The long-haired Goff produces lots of wool.
The short-haired Goff produces good quality meat.

(a) (i) What has caused the two breeds to be different?

cross breeding g Evolution

0

(ii) Give **two** environmental factors which might affect meat quality
or wool production.

1 *Pollution*

2 *not enough food*

1

2 marks

(b) Scientists decide to mate a long-haired Goff with a short-haired Goff.
They want to produce a sheep with good wool and meat.

(i) Scientists often use this process of deliberately mating different
breeds to produce offspring with certain characteristics.
What is this process called?

Selective breeding

1

1 mark

(ii) As well as high quality meat and wool, give **one** other characteristic
farmers might want sheep to have.

Be big g - long lif
- high growth rate
- resistance to
disease

0

1 mark

maximum 5 marks

SHP3U

Coordination Group Publications

Key Stage 3
Science

Answer Book

SATS Practice Papers
Levels 5-7

Contents

These practice papers won't make you better at Science

... but they will show you what you **can** do, and what you **can't** do.

The papers are just like the ones you'll get on the day — so they'll tell you what you need to **work at** if you want to do **better**.

Do a test, **mark it** and look at what you **got wrong**.
That's the stuff you need to learn.

Go away, **learn** those tricky bits, then **do the <u>same</u> test again**. If you're **still** getting questions wrong, you'll have to do even **more practice** and **keep testing** yourself until you get all the questions right.

It doesn't sound like a lot of **fun**, but how else do you expect to **learn** it?

There are two big ways to improve your score

1) **Keep practising the things you get wrong**
   If you keep getting the energy questions wrong, practise energy. If you keep making a hash of the plants questions, practise plants. And so on...

2) **Don't throw away easy marks**
   Even if a question looks dead simple you have to check your answer and make sure it's sensible.

Doing the Tests

There are **three sets** of practice papers in this pack.

Each set has:

Test A
1 hour test   **75 marks**

Test B
1 hour test   **75 marks**

Follow all the instructions

1)   The most important thing is to **understand** the questions.
     Read everything really **carefully** to be sure you're doing what they want.

2)   If you're going to do the practice papers more than once,
     then write your answers on a separate bit of paper.

Working out your Grade

- Do a complete exam (paper A and paper B).

- Mark both exam papers, and add up the marks (which gives you a mark out of 150).

- Look it up in this table to see what grade you got.

Mark	150 – 105	104 – 73	72 – 42	41 – 36	under 36
Level	**7**	**6**	**5**	**4**	**N**

Important

Getting Level 4, 5, 6 or 7 on one of these practice papers is **no guarantee**
of getting that in the real SAT — **but** it is a pretty good guide.

Q	Marks	Correct answer	Useful tips
1. a	1	Minerals	
b	1	Big surface area **OR** They stretch deeper **OR** Covers a large area.	
c	1	The tree can't photosynthesise **OR** No food is produced.	
d	2	It's camouflaged (**OR** It looks like a twig **OR** It's the same colour **OR** pattern as a twig) **OR** Birds can't see it. **Any two things, one mark each.**	
2. a (i)	1	300 ml	
(ii)	3	More carbon dioxide, more water vapour, less oxygen. **One mark for each.**	
b (i)	1	Trachea **OR** Wind pipe	
(ii)	1	The rings stop the trachea collapsing **OR** To support the trachea **OR** To keep the trachea open.	
3. a	1	1975	
b	1	'It affects the nervous system.' **should be circled.**	
c (i)	2	The chance of having an accident increase, the rate of increase gets faster the more alcohol is in the blood. **One mark for just saying 'it increases'.**	
(ii)	1	'Alcohol increases the time it takes for a person to react'. **should be circled.**	
4. a	2	Light from the lamp shines on the cup and is scattered **OR** reflected. **One mark.** Some of the light travels to Suzanne's eyes and she sees the cup. **One mark.**	
b	2	The blank boxes of the table should read, 'red — blue' **One mark for each.**	
c	1	Black absorbs all light. **OR** It doesn't scatter any light.	
d (i)	1	30°	
(ii)	1	30°	
(iii)	1	2.5 cm	
(iv)	1	2.5 cm	
5. a	2	Potassium, zinc, nickel, platinum. **One mark for getting zinc and nickel the wrong way round.**	
b (i)	1	Sodium	*TIP: Bleugh, reactivity series. This is hard but there will be a question on it. There's no doubt about it, you've got to learn it.*
(ii)	1	Hydrogen	
c (i)	1	Platinum	
(ii)	1	Zinc is less reactive than potassium so it does not replace it in the salt.	
6. a	1	120 N	
b	1	The force from the string is not balanced **OR** It is pushed by the string **OR** Potential energy is converted to kinetic energy **OR** Energy is transferred to the arrow from the bow.	
c	1	They are at right angles to each other **OR** They are in perpendicular directions	
d	1	It would have a larger surface area **OR** Because pressure is force divided by area	
7. a	1	It is the furthest from the Sun.	
b	2	**Mercury:** The temperature is +170 °C so water would boil away. **One mark.** **Mars:** The temperature is -55 °C so water would be frozen. **One mark.**	*TIP: This is an easy question — just make sure you read the table carefully.*
c	1	Jupiter	
d	1	Gravity	
e	2	The planets reflect light **[One mark]** from the Sun **[One mark]**.	
8. a	1	The hairs sweep (**OR** move/push/waft) the egg along the oviduct.	
b	1	A sperm cell has a tail to provide movement **OR** It is a streamlined shape **OR** It contains enzymes **OR** It contains half the number of chromosomes.	
c	2	The mother's blood and the baby's blood pass close to each other **[One mark]** in the placenta **[One mark]** so food can pass to the baby along the umbilical cord. **[One mark]** **Maximum two marks.**	

Q	Marks	Correct answer	Useful tips
9. a (i)	2	Minerals and vitamins. **One mark for each.**	
(ii)	1	Fibre	
b	1	To keep the tube at a constant temperature **OR** To control the temperature.	*TIP: Part (e) is just common sense. There's no trick to it.*
c	1	All the protein had been digested **OR** There was no starch left	
d	1	At 30 °C, the protease digests the protein faster.	
e	1	Use the same equipment and quantities. **Other answers possible.**	
10. a	1	C	
b	1	A	
c	1	All of the liquid had evaporated.	
d	1	22 °C	
e	2	The temperatures would not be so low **One mark** The temperatures would start to go back up sooner. **One mark**	
11. a	3	The sedimentary rocks were formed by sediment laid down in the river channels on Mars. The igneous rocks were formed from molten lava pushed up from Mars' volcanoes. The pressure from the mountains on rocks underneath changes them – these are metamorphic rocks. **One mark for each (wording may differ).**	
b	2	The rocks will break up (**OR** split up **OR** be weathered). **One mark.** The severe temperature changes will cause expanding and contracting in the rocks. **One mark.**	
12. a	1	'kinetic energy' **should be circled.**	
b	2	Friction between the wheel and the stand means some energy is lost as heat. Some of the energy is lost as sound from the wheel and the dynamo going round. Some energy is lost as heat in the wires. **One mark for each point, maximum two marks. Other answers possible.**	*TIP: This is tricky. You need to think it through and <u>explain</u> yourself well.*
c	2	The wheel slows down quicker. **One mark** The turning wheel has the same amount of energy to transfer as in part. (b) **OR** The energy is transferred quicker. **One mark**	
13. a	2	$40 \times 0.5 = 20$ Nm **One mark for answer without unit.**	
b	1	$20 \div 0.2 = 100$ N **Accept answer to (a) ÷ 0.2.**	
c (i)	2	$0.5 \ cm^2 = 0.5 \div 10\ 000 \ m^2$, P = F / A = 80 / 0.00005 = 1 600 000 Pa or Nm^{-2} **One mark for answer without unit.** **OR** P = $80 \div 0.5 = 160 \ Ncm^{-2}$ **One mark.**	
(ii)	1	Make the handle longer **OR** Decrease distance from pivot to the rod **OR** Reduce the surface area of the peg. **Other answers possible.**	

Q	Marks	Correct answer	Useful tips
1. a	2	The turbine converts wind energy to kinetic energy.	TIPS: Two words for you, renewable energy — learn it.
		The generator converts kinetic energy to electrical energy.	
		One mark for each	
b	1	The wind can not be used up.	
c	2	Tidal energy **OR** Solar power **OR** Biomass **OR** Hydroelectric **OR** Geothermal. **One mark each for any two of these.**	
d	2	Ads: More controllable, it may not be windy **OR** Oil powered can be built anywhere. **One mark for either.**	
		Disads: Oil is non-renewable **OR** Oil causes more pollution. **One mark for either.**	

2. a	1	Sun to the left of the Earth, in a line with it and the Moon.	
b	3	Sun. **One mark.**	
		Earth. **One mark.**	
		Sun.	
		Moon. **One mark for Sun and Moon.**	
c	1	The Earth spins on its axis so each part faces the Sun.	
d	1	Anti-Clockwise.	

3. a	1	Metal 2. *(Because the metal at the bottom expands more quickly and makes the strip bend upwards.)*	
b	1	Steel. *(Steel gives the biggest difference in expansion rates.)*	
c (i)	1	The strip straightens. This breaks the contact again and the fan turns off.	
(ii)	1	The more the screw is moved down, the less the strip needs to bend to complete the circuit, so the fan comes on at a lower temperature.	

4. a	1	C. *(There is no change in movement so the forces must be balanced.)*	TIPS: Unbalanced forces lead to a change in movement. If the object is staying still, or moving in the same way, the forces are balanced.
b	1	A. *(There is a change in speed. It is going up faster so the overall force must be up.)*	
c	1	B. *(There is a change in speed.)*	
		(The force down is slowing it down so it is greater than the tension pulling it up.)	
d	1	C. *(There is no change in speed or direction so the forces must be balanced.)*	

5. a (i)	1	Copper Oxide. *(It is left over because no more could dissolve.)*	
(ii)	1	Copper Sulphate.	
b	1	Copper oxide + Sulphuric acid ➔ Copper sulphate.	
c	1	To remove the undissolved copper oxide.	

6. a	2	Nitrogen, Carbon, Oxygen **One mark for two right.**	
b	1	Carbon dioxide **OR** Sulphur dioxide **OR** Copper oxide **OR** Carbon monoxide. **One mark for any one of these.**	
c	1	Carbon dioxide **and** Carbon monoxide.	TIPS: An element is just one thing. Compounds are more than one combined.
d	1	Carbon dioxide.	
e	1	Nitrogen	
f	1	Sulphur dioxide	

7. a (i)	2	Protein, Fat, Vitamins. **One mark each for any 2 of these.**	
(ii)	2	Fibre **and** Water. **One mark for each.**	
b	2	Carbohydrate, Minerals. **One mark for each.**	
c	2	To break down the cells **OR** To mix the food with saliva and begin digestion **OR**	
		Increase surface area of food **OR** Make swallowing easier. **One mark each for any two of these.**	

8. a (i)	1	Plant.	
(ii)	2	It has chloroplasts **OR** Has starch grains **OR** Has a cell wall. **One mark each for any two of these even if (i) incorrect.**	
b	2	Produces glucose for energy. **One mark for glucose and one for its use as energy.**	

Q	Marks	Correct answer	Useful tips
9. a	3	20 Nm. *$100 \times 0.2 = 20$ Nm.* **One mark for working, one for units, one for answer.**	*TIPS: When you do these mathsy questions you've got to remember the units.*
b (i)	1	20 Nm. *(It balances the moment of the 100 N force.)*	
(ii)	1	25 N. *$20 \div 0.8 = 25$ N.*	
(iii)	2	20 N/cm^2. *$100 \div 5 = 20$ N/cm^2.* **One mark for units, one for answer.**	

Q	Marks	Correct answer	Useful tips
10. a	1	The volume of water to be heated was less in flask B.	
b	1	Flask A: 39 °C. Flask B: 52 °C. *(The blocks and the water reach the same temperature.)*	
c	2	The block in Flask A. **[One mark]** Because its temperature dropped more. **[One mark]**	

Q	Marks	Correct answer	Useful tips
11. a (i)	1	The distance gets smaller.	
(ii)	1	The distance stays the same.	
(iii)	1	The pressure increases.	*TIPS: Gases compress much more easily than liquids — and have you tried compressing a solid.*
(iv)	1	The volume of air reduces.	
b	2	More water moves in and so it becomes less buoyant. The sub has an increased density when filled with water. **One mark for each.**	

Q	Marks	Correct answer	Useful tips
12. a (i)	1	It is difficult for the water to seep through **OR** Water runs off **OR** evaporates. **One mark for either.**	
(ii)	1	Difficult for the tree's roots to grow **OR** Difficult for nutrients and minerals to reach the tree. **One mark for either.**	
b	2	For photosynthesis **OR** For transport **OR** For growth **OR** To make the plant firm. **One mark for each of two of these.**	
c (i)	1	Increased surface area **OR** Allow water to seep through easily **OR** To stop trench falling in. **One mark for either.**	
(ii)	1	Make protein **OR** Make amino acids. **One mark for either.**	

Q	Marks	Correct answer	Useful tips
13.	1	O$_2$	
	2	Water H$_2$O Compound **One mark for 2 out of the 3.**	
	1	Element	*TIPS: There's only one thing more important than checking your answers — checking them again.*
	1	Copper	
	1	Sodium	
	1	Carbon **OR** graphite	

Q	Marks	Correct answer	Useful tips

1. a | 1 | Filtration

b | 1 | As a control **OR** To show it's the dissolved substances that affect it

c (i) | 1 | Minerals **OR** salts **OR** nutrients

(ii) | 1 | Root hairs **OR** Large surface area **OR** They spread out

d | 1 | The leaves need light for photosynthesis.

2. a | 1 | 130 °C

b (i) | 1 | B

(ii) | 1 | D

c (i) | 1 | 0 minutes and 5 minutes

(ii) | 1 | 10 minutes and 15 minutes

TIP: The stuff you need to know is easy for this question — just take care reading the graph...

3. a | 2 | Blue – It changes colour in both acid and alkali. **1 mark only without explanation.**

b | 1 | Chromatography

c | 3 | Dissolved — solvent — green **One mark for each.**

4. a | 1 | ... will produce the most violent reaction when reacting with water. (Also accept: ... will fizz the most **or** ... will produce gas the quickest

b | 1 | 3 - 1 - 2 - 5 - 4

c | 1 | 3

d | 1 | Bubble gas into inverted measuring cylinder and time how long it takes to produce a certain volume of gas (or any sensible answer)

TIP: Reactivity series always comes up — you'd be a loony not to learn it...

5. a | 1 | Distillation

b | 1 | 100 °C

c | 1 | It condenses the water vapour.

d | 4 | **1** Condensing **2** Boiling **OR** Evaporating **3** Melting **4** Freezing

e | 1 | *in piece of apparatus labelled X* 1   *in the flask containing impure water* 2   **Both required for one mark.**

6. a (i) | 1 | Refraction

(ii) | 1 | It is reflected **OR** It is scattered **OR** It bounces off **OR** It is absorbed by the air

b | 1 | **Top to bottom reads:** red green blue **violet**

c | 1 | 'The red part of the spectrum stays the same, but the other colours disappear.' **should be ticked.**

7. a | 1 | Plant material **OR** Material from living things

b | 1 | The Sun

c | 2 | Natural gas (**OR** Gas **OR** Methane), Coal, Oil **One mark for two right.**

d | 1 | They can't be replaced **OR** No more can be made after they are used up

e (i) | 1 | There is more energy per unit mass **OR** It takes up less space **OR** It can be used in vehicles

(ii) | 1 | It is renewable **OR** It is widely available

(iii) | 1 | They release greenhouses gases **OR** Pollution **OR any example of a specific pollutant (eg: CO$_2$) being released.**

8. a | 1 | Mercury **OR** Venus

b | 1 | It rotates **OR** spins **OR** turns on its axis

c | 1 | Its axis is tilted **OR** Sometimes one pole is closer to the Sun than the other

d | 2 | The year is how long the planet takes to orbit the Sun. **One mark**.
The further the planet is from the Sun, the greater the distance it has to travel **OR** the slower it travels in its orbit so the longer it takes. **One mark**.

Q	Marks	Correct answer	Useful tips
9. a	1	resistant to the disease **OR** will not catch the disease **OR** has antibodies against the disease	
b	1	Antibodies	
c	1	Dead virus / bacteria / microorganism **OR** Mild strain of bacteria / virus **OR** antigens **Other answers possible.**	
d	1	Antibodies pass to the baby via the placenta **OR** breast milk.	
e	1	It goes down and stays down **OR** It continues downwards **OR** Few people got measles after 1970	
f	1	It will increase **OR** It will go back up to the levels before 1970	
10. a	1	The water molecules move faster / further apart **OR** They have more energy	
b	1	The water expanded as it froze / became a solid **OR** The pressure in the bulb increased as the water froze	
c	1	No – the water will boil / evaporate OR water boils at 100 °C	
d	1	'Volume of the bulb increased before the water expanded.' **should be circled.**	
11. a	1	250 kJ **1400 – 790 – 160 – 200 = 250**	
b	1	Growing **OR** For storing **OR** For producing meat **OR** For making the chicken fatter	
c	2	**glucose +** oxygen → water + carbon dioxide **One mark for oxygen, one mark for water and carbon dioxide.**	
d	1	Stop them moving **OR** Keep them warm **OR** Keep them close together	*TIPS: Learn this, do this, write that, nag, nag, nag.*
e	2	Less food is needed. More energy is available for making eggs **OR** growth. The farmer will get larger hens **OR** more meat. The farmer will get more eggs **OR** larger eggs. **Any two of these, one mark each.**	
12. a	1	To replace the vitamins / minerals that are used up **OR** People use up the vitamins / minerals	
b	2	**Zn** Zinc **Fe** Iron **One mark each.**	*TIP: They won't ask you about dodgy element names. No one can remember the symbol for tungsten for crying out loud…*
c	1	Rb	
13. a (i)	1	**Both required for one mark.**	
(ii)	1	**Arrow must be drawn inside the tube.**	
(iii)	1	North	
b	1	Connect the battery the other way round **OR** Reverse the direction of the electricity **OR** Wind the coil the other way round	
c (i)	1		
(ii)	1	They attract each other	
14. a	1	It vibrates with a higher frequency **OR** It vibrates more quickly	
b	1	It vibrates with a greater amplitude.	
c	1	They can burst the ear drum **OR** They can damage the nerve ending / cochlea / bones in the ear	

Q	Marks	Correct answer	Useful tips

1. a (i) | 1 | Larger than the drag. *[The forward force must be more to make the bike speed up.]*

(ii) | 1 | Equal to the drag. *[The movement is staying the same so the forces are balanced.]*

(iii) | 1 | Less than the drag. *[The drag must be more to slow the bike down.]*

b (i) | 1 | The molecules collide with the bike **OR** They take away energy from the bike

(ii) | 2 | Larger. There are more collisions. **One mark for each**

c | 1 | Friction

2. a | 1 | Venus

b | 1 | B

c | 1 | D

d | 1 | 1 year

e | 1 | **Any answer between 100 and 300 days**

f | 1 | Jupiter.

3. a | 1 | The motor runs backwards. *The current goes the other way around the circuit.*

b | 1 | The batteries / wire get hot **OR** The batteries go flat quickly **OR**
It shorts out the batteries.

c | 1 | The motor would not run.

d (i) | 1 | No change. *The current doesn't flow through the resistor so it has no effect.*

(ii) | 1 | The motor turns but more slowly than before. *If resistance goes up, current must go down.*

e | 1 | Change the direction of one of the cells. **Other answers possible.**

4. a | 2 |

Completed diagram should be similar to this.
One mark for the ray inside the prism, drawn as shown.
One mark for the ray to the screen, drawn as shown.

b (i) | 1 | Spectrum **OR** Rainbow effect.

(ii) | 1 | Just the blue of the spectrum **OR** Only blue light

(iii) | 1 | It absorbs all the other colours, only letting blue light through.

5. a (i) | 1 | 4

(ii) | 1 | 3

(iii) | 1 | Sedimentary

(iv) | 1 | 3 *Granite is an igneous rock.*

b | 2 | Calcium chloride + Carbon dioxide. **1 mark for each.**

c | 1 | No reaction. *Otherwise it would react with test tubes.*

6. a | 2 | pH probe should be ticked (Universal indicator paper is no good for obtaining pH measurements to one d.p.).
Two marks for only pH probe ticked. One mark for universal indicator paper and pH probe both ticked.

b | 1 | Repeat the tests to see if both sets of results agree.

c | 1 | 1

d | 1 | Neutralisation.

e | 1 | 5

7. a | 1 | 1.03g *27.32 – 26.29 = 1.03g.*

b (i) | 1 | Magnesium + Oxygen ➜ Magnesium oxide.

(ii) | 1 | The magnesium gains oxygen from the air.

Q	Marks	Correct answer	Useful tips
8. a	1	25-30 **OR** The last 5 weeks	*The graph gets steeper and steeper so the most growth is in the last weeks on the graph.*
b	1	Supports the foetus **OR** Allows the foetus to grow and move **OR** Cushions the foetus	
c	4	Air goes into the mother's lungs. Oxygen diffuses into her blood. It is transported in her blood to the placenta. It diffuses across the placenta into the blood of the foetus. It is transported to the cells of the foetus via the umbilical cord. It diffuses into the cells of the foetus. **One mark for each, maximum four marks.**	
9. a (i)	2	Both rods become magnetised. They roll apart because like poles repel. **One mark for each.**	
(ii)	1	The rods remain magnetised so they stay apart.	
b	2	Nothing will happen. The wooden rod can't be magnetised. **One mark for each.**	
10. a	1	The card vibrates.	
b	1	The pitch gets higher.	*TIPS: Vibrations cause a sound, the faster the vibration the higher the pitch of the note, simple.*
c (i)	1	Kinetic energy changes into heat and sound energy.	
(ii)	1	The pitch gets lower.	
11. a	1		
b (i)	1	Mg	*TIPS: The periodic table is as important to science as vinegar is to chips. So make sure you know all about it.*
(ii)	1	C	
c (i)	1	Sodium chloride.	
(ii)	1	Magnesium sulphide.	
d	1	Table salt **OR** Salt	
e	1	Oxygen **OR** Hydrogen **OR** Nitrogen **OR** Fluorine **OR** Chlorine	
f	1	Sodium **OR** Na	
12. a (i)	1	Photosynthesis	
(ii)	1	Oxygen	
(iii)	1	Carbon dioxide	
(iv)	1	Respiration	*TIPS: You think you're bored, you should try writing these papers.*
b	2	There are no insects or other animals to transfer pollen. There is no wind to transfer pollen. **One mark for each.**	
c	1	To make protein / amino acids	
d	1	Phosphorus **OR** potassium	
13. a	1	A	
b	1	C	
c	1	B	
d	1	D	

Q	Marks	Correct answer	Useful tips
1. a	1	red blood cell.	
b (i)	1	1.	
(ii)	1	5.	*TIPS: Wakey, wakey...*
c	1	testicle **OR** testis **One mark for either**	
d	1	root **OR** root epidermis **One mark for any one of these**	

2. a	2	the weeds shaded the radish plants **OR** the weeds left the radish plants less space to grow **OR** the weeds took (most of) the available water **OR** the weeds took (most of) the available minerals/nutrients **One mark for each, up to 2 marks. No mark for 'the radish plants had less space' or 'weeds took the food'**	
b	3	(more) photosynthesis took place **OR** plants made more food **One mark** (more) carbohydrate (**OR** sugar **OR** glucose) was made in the leaves **One mark. No mark for 'food was made in the leaves'.** (more) carbohydrate (**OR** sugar **OR** glucose) was transported to (**OR** stored in) the roots **One mark**	

3. a	2	it keeps it cool **OR** it gets shade **OR** it hides it from the sun stops it drying out protects (**OR** hides) it from predators it cannot be seen by its prey **One mark for each, up to 2 marks. No mark for 'it finds water' OR 'hides it' OR 'conserves the snake's energy'.**	
b	2	crushes/damages it **OR** crushes/damages organs prevents breathing **OR** suffocates it **OR** chokes it **OR** strangles it prevents/reduces blood flow to organs **OR** stops blood flowing **One mark for each, up to 2 marks. No mark for 'causes a heart attack'.**	*TIPS: This question is about how animals adapt to make them good at what they do. Why do rabbits have strong back legs, elephants have big ears and all that stuff. The examiners love it — so give 'em what they want.*

4. a	4	monthly cycle; the uterus; an ovary; the middle. **One mark for each**	
b	2	growth spurt; start to produce sperm; growth of testicles/testes; growth of penis; increase in body hair; increase in facial hair; voice gets deeper **One mark for each, up to 2 marks**	
c	1	Hormones	

5. a	1	Attrition **OR** Erosion. **One mark for each**	*TIPS: All this stuff about rocks might seem like geography, but it's a very popular science question every year.*
b	2	They are smoothed and rounded. They get smaller. **One mark for each**	
c	1	Stage 4: Deposition / Sedimentation.	
	1	Stage 5: Compression/Compaction.	

6. a	1	It goes up as the temperature rises **OR** It goes down as it gets colder **OR** It dissolves more at higher temperatures **One mark for any one of these**	
b (i)	1	74	
(ii)	1	24	
c	2	Because water freezes at 0°C **(One mark)** and boils at 100°C **(One mark)**	

7. a	3		**One mark** — *for a ray from brick to eye, bending at the surface of the water and not passing through the side of the pool.* **One mark** — *for accurately drawing the correct ray: must touch the brick and eye, must be a continuous ray and must be drawn with a ruler [only award this mark if the first mark has been given].* **One mark** — *for an arrow showing that the light enters the eye.*
b	1	Refraction	
c	2	It only allows blue light through **AND** It absorbs all the colours except blue **One mark for each.**	

8. a	1	Venus **OR** Mercury **One mark for either.**	
b	1	Mars **OR** Jupiter **OR** Saturn **OR** Uranus **OR** Neptune **OR** Pluto **One mark for any of these.**	
c	1	The Earth spins on its axis.	
d			*TIPS: Stuff about planets and orbits is pretty straightforward. We're spinning around and spinning around the Sun at the same time — dizzying stuff, but lots of marks.*
	1	It takes 1 year to go all the way around the Sun. 9 months is 3/4 year so it's 3/4 of the way around.	

© CGP 2002

Q	Marks	Correct answer	Useful tips
9. a	1	They expand.	
b	1	They shrink.	
c	1	They might buckle or crack **OR** Slip over each other. **One mark for either.**	
d	1	It can be squashed, allowing the concrete to expand.	

10. a

	1	Up: Less voles leaves more grass and trees for the mice to eat.	
	1	Down: Less voles means owls eat more mice.	

b

| 1 | |

fleas
foxes
rabbits
grass

TIPS: Remember that these are pyramids of numbers. So even though fleas are tiny they get a big block balanced on top of the pyramid. That's just 'cos there's loads of them.

Q	Marks	Correct answer
11. a (i)	1	an enzyme **OR** pepsin **OR** protease
(ii)	1	it's the temperature that enzymes work best **OR** it's the temperature of the body
		No mark for 'this is body heat' or 'to make a fair test'
b (i)	1	growth **OR** repair **OR** making other proteins/enzymes **OR** to supply amino acids **No mark for 'energy'**
(ii)	1	They pass through the intestine wall **OR** are absorbed/pass into the blood **OR** pass through gut wall.
	1	They're carried by the blood/plasma/bloodstream **OR** they go through blood vessels/arteries/veins.
c	1	To kill microbes/bacteria.

Q	Marks	Correct answer
12. a	2	as chemical energy **[One mark]** in Matt's muscles **[One mark]**
b	1	the molecules hit the walls of the balloon **OR** they bounce off the walls/balloon
c	1	they speed up/get faster
d	1	they'll hit the wall of the balloon more often/harder/faster **OR** more collisions with balloon
		No mark for 'more collisions' or 'molecules move faster'
e	1	there will be more frequent collisions with the wall of the balloon **OR** more collisions with the balloon **OR** the force applied by the molecules increases **OR** the surface tension in the rubber will be greater.
		No mark for 'more collisions' or 'less space for molecules' or 'there are more air molecules to hit the balloon wall'

13.

Q	Marks	Correct answer
a	1	2 4 1 **One mark if all 3 numbers are present in correct order**
b	1	oxygen
c	1	hydrogen
d	1	it (is the only one which) forms an acidic oxide **No mark for 'it burns to give an acid'**
e	1	sodium **OR** potassium **OR** lithium **OR** barium **OR** caesium **OR** rubidium **OR** calcium
		No mark for 'aluminium,' or 'magnesium'

TIPS: Properties of metals and the like are just a few simple facts to learn and it'll be worth it in the exam. Don't say I didn't warn you.

14.

Q	Marks	Correct answer
a	2	96 Nm **One mark for 96, one mark for Nm (OR can be 9600 Ncm)**
b	2	12 m/s **One mark for 12, one mark for m/s (OR can be 1200 cm/s)**
c	1	the same as **OR** equal to **OR** same **(No mark for 'similar')**
	1	less than **OR** less **OR** lower **(No mark for 'weaker' or 'half')**
d	1	300 Hz **No mark if more than one frequency circled**
e	1	chemical/potential energy in the bell-ringer **OR** chemical energy **No mark for 'energy in the bell-ringer'**
	1	transferred via the rope/mechanically **OR** transferred to the bell **OR** transferred from the rope **OR** to the rope **OR** potential/kinetic energy in the bell **No mark for 'to kinetic energy,' or 'to potential energy'**
	1	as bell swings, kinetic energy changes to potential energy **OR** as bell swings, potential energy changes to kinetic energy **No mark for if the bell swinging is not mentioned**
	1	transferred by sound **OR** becomes sound energy **OR** transferred to surroundings/sound/the air/people's ears
		One mark for each of the four potential points, BUT with a maximum of 3 marks. The points must be made in a logical order.

TIPS: Moments and energy transfer in all their glory in one question. So make sure you've got the answers right. If not practise and practise again 'cos it'll be in the exam.

3B KS3 Levels 5-7 Science Paper 3B

Q	Marks	Correct answer	Useful tips

1. a (i) | 1 | The more weight, the more bags of sugar are needed. |
(ii) | 1 | 10 bags. *The number of bags increases by 2 for each 1N. So for an extra ½N add 1 bag.* |
b (i) | 1 | He will need fewer bags. |
(ii) | 1 | Add a lubricant such as washing-up liquid or oil to the table. |

2. a | 2 | They reflect light **[One mark]** from the Sun **[One mark]**. |
b | 1 | The Earth moves between the Sun and the satellite **OR** the satellite moves into the Earth's shadow. |
c | 1 | Weather prediction **OR** Navigation **OR** Communication **OR** Spying **OR** Astronomy. |

3. | 1 | No   No   Zero   **All three correct for one mark** |
 | 2 | No   No   Zero   **All three correct for two marks** |
 | 2 | Yes   No   +ve   **All three correct for two marks** |

TIPS: Circuit diagrams come up a lot. You just need to think about how the current moves around the circuit.

4. a | 1 | Keeps them warm. |
 | 2 | Camouflages them and protects them from predators. **One mark for camouflage, one for explanation.** |
b (i) | 1 | DNA |
(ii) | 1 | Sperm. |
(iii) | 1 | Nuclei **OR** Nucleus. |
(iv) | 1 | Inherit. |

5. a | 1 | Small dark flecks of iron will be seen on the magnet **OR** Iron would be attracted to the magnet. |
b | 2 | Iron compounds are not magnetic **OR** Iron is one element, a compound contains more than one element chemically combined (**OR** Any other valid comparison of conductivity, colour, rusting). **One mark for any of these up to 2 marks.** |
c | 2 | Iron chloride + Hydrogen. |
d | 2 | Can't carry as much oxygen around the body. They need oxygen to produce energy. **One mark for each.** |

6. a | 2 | Use the same weight of crisps and snack **OR** Use the same amount of; and starting temperature of; water **OR** Keep the same distance of crisp or snack to the test tube. **One mark for any of these up to 2 marks.** |
b | 2 | Wear goggles **OR** Point the test tube away from him **OR** Light the food at arm's length. **One mark each for any 2.** |
c | 1 | A. *Because they have a higher energy content.* |
d (i) | 1 | Fibre is not digested by the body. |
(ii) | 1 | Provides a hard substance to clean out the digestive system. |
(iii) | 2 | Lower in fat. Higher in fibre. **One mark for each.** |
e | 1 | Oranges **OR** peas **OR** beans **OR** lemons. *(other answers possible)* **One mark for any one of these.** |

TIPS: Learn the basic bits you need for a balanced diet. It might well come up in the exam, and if it doesn't, you might live longer anyway.

7. a | 3 |

Nucleus — Cell Membrane — Cytoplasm **One mark for each.**

TIPS: The basic structure of animal and plant cells are easy enough and often come up in the exam. So stick them in your head.

b | 2 | Cell wall **OR** Vacuole **OR** Chloroplasts. **One mark for any of these up to 2 marks.** |
c | 1 | Tissue **OR** organ |

8. a (i) | 1 | 30 m. *Lamp posts are 10 metres apart. 3 × 10 = 30 m.* |
(ii) | 1 | 3 m/s. *30 m in 10 seconds. 30 ÷ 10 = 3 m/s.* |
b | 1 | 105 m. *35 seconds at 3 m/s. 35 × 3 = 105 m.* |
c | 1 | The light from the flash reflects off Denise and other objects and returns to the camera. |

Q	Marks	Correct answer	Useful tips
9. a (i)	1	Iron and Sulphur. **One mark only if both are correct.**	
b (ii)	1	Copper oxide	*TIPS: You're going to need to know your compounds from your elements — and your arms from your elbow.*
(ii)	2	Acid rain **OR** Causes leaf fall **OR** Affects breathing **OR** Weathers buildings **OR** Poisons aquatic organisms **One mark for any of these up to 2 marks.**	
(iii)	1	Alkaline.	
c	2	E.g. Use: electrical wires. Property: good electrical conductor **OR** easily drawn into wires. Use: cooking pots. Property: good conductor of heat. **Other answers possible. One mark for a suitable use, one mark for a relevant property.**	
10. a (i)	1	Iron **OR** Nickel **OR** steel **OR** Cobalt *(other answers possible)* **One mark for any one of these.**	
(ii)	1	Iron **OR** Nickel **OR** steel **OR** Cobalt *(other answers possible)* **One mark for any one of these.**	
b	3	The core becomes magnetised The arm is attracted to the core This tips the arm about the pivot and pushes the contact together. **One mark for each part of the explanation.**	*TIPS: If a question is worth 3 marks, they probably want 3 points in your answer, drrr.*
c	1	Because the contacts are together current still flows around the coil and the core remains magnetised. Therefore the core continues to attract the arm which keeps pushing the contacts together.	
11. a (i)	2	CO_2 **OR** H_2O **OR** CO **OR** C. **One mark for any of these up to 2 marks.**	
(ii)	2	Water droplets on the jar **OR** Soot **OR** Light / heat given off. **One mark for any of these up to 2 marks.**	
b (i)	2	The carbon dioxide level decreases. The oxygen level rises.	*TIPS: If you find you're running out of time in these practice papers think about how long you spend on each question. Don't spend ages on one question, especially if it's only worth a mark or two. Get on with the rest and come back to it later.*
(ii)	2	Photosynthesis stops. Respiration continues **OR** The changes would reverse. **One mark for each.**	
c (i)	1	Chloroplasts.	
(ii)	1	Nucleus.	
12. a (i)	1	Evolution **OR** They have inherited different characteristics **OR** They have different genes. **One mark for any of these.**	
(ii)	2	Weather conditions **OR** Availability of food and water **OR** Levels of disease. **One mark for any of these up to 2 marks.**	
b (i)	1	Selective breeding.	
(ii)	1	Hardiness **OR** Long life **OR** Fertility **OR** High growth rate **OR** Resistance to disease. **One mark for any of these.**	